JAMVA CHALOJI

Dedicated to my great-grandmother
Soonamai Kanjibhai Patel
of Tadgaon

I would like her to know
how much I appreciated all I saw
and learnt in her presence by
the kitchen fire.

JAMVA CHALOJI
PARSI DELICACIES FOR ALL OCCASIONS

KATY DALAL

VAKILS, FEFFER AND SIMONS PVT. LTD.
Hague Building, 9, Sprott Road,
Ballard Estate, Mumbai 400 001.

First printing 1998
Second printing 1999
Third printing 2002

Price: Rs. 195/-

Published by Bimal Mehta for
Vakils, Feffer and Simons Pvt. Ltd., Hague Building,
9, Sprott Road, Ballard Estate, Mumbai 400 001.

Printed by Arun K. Mehta at Vakil & Sons Pvt. Ltd.,
Industry Manor, 2nd Floor, Appasaheb Marathe Marg,
Prabhadevi, Mumbai 400 025.

Cover Photograph

Patra-Ni-Macchi	9
Tareli Kolmi	54
Lili Chutney Bharela Chhamna	41

ISBN 81-87111-06-2

CONTENTS

The Parsi Lagan-nu-Bhonu x

Introduction xi

Historical Introduction xii

The Parsi Wedding Feast

Rotli 1

Gajar-Mewa-Nu-Achaar 1
(Carrot and Dried Fruit Pickle)

Macchi-No-Sahas 2
([Method 1] Fish Sauce – with Rice Flour)

Macchi-No-Sahas 2
([Method 2] Fish Sauce – with Gram Flour)

Marghi-Na-Farcha (Fried Chicken) 3

Lagan-Na-Tarkari-per-Eda (Wedding style Eggs .....
on Tomatoes and Coriander) 4

Lagan-Nu-Custard (Wedding Custard) 4

Keri-Nu-Icecream (Mango Ice-cream) 5

Malai-Na-Paratha (Malai Parathas) 5

Gos-No-Pulao (Mutton Pulao) 6

Bapaiji Ni Dhansakh Ni Dar 7
(Traditional Parsi Dal)

Dodhi–No–Murambo (White Pumpkin Halwa) 7

Sali-Ne-Jardaloo-Ma-Gos (Sweet and Sour
Mutton Gravy with Apricots and Potato
Shoestrings) 8

Lagan-Nu-Achaar (Wedding Pickle) 9

Patra-Ni-Macchi (Fish in Banana Leaves) 9

Shirazi Pulao 10
(Saffron, Mutton And Dried Fruit Pulao)

Kesar-Pista Kulfi (Saffron-Pistachio Kulfi) 11

Sali-Ma-Marghi (Chicken with potato
shoestring) 12

Parsi Sev (Sweet Vermicelli) 12

Mitthoo Dahi (Sweet Curd) 13

Dhan-Dar (White Rice, and Yellow Dal) 13

Chamna-Ne-Kolmi-No-Patio 14
(Prawn And Pomfret Patia)

Bharuchi Akoori 15
(Savoury Scrambled Eggs with Nuts)

Sado Ravo (Simple Semolina) 15

Ravo (Sweet Semolina) 16

Sweet Hot Tea With Lemon Grass,
Fresh Peppermint And Mint 16

Sweet Dishes

Malido 17

Shirinbai Panthaky No Eda No Malido 17
(Shrinbai Panthaky's Malido)

Khaman-Na-Ladwa 18
(Cornflour Coconut Laddoos)

Rice Kheer 19

Chokha Ni Kheer (Rice Kheer) 19

Kheer-Kesar-Ni (Saffron Kheer) 20

Ghehu-Nu-Dudh (Wheat-Milk Sweet) 20

Falooda 21

Tal-Na-Ladwa (Sesame Laddoos) 22

Soothanoo (Dried Ginger Sweet) 22

Saalam Paak (Milk Sweet) 23

Gajjar-No-Halwo (Carrot Halwa) 23

Gajjar-No-Murambo 24
(Carrot Marmalade)

Dodhi–No–Halwo 24
(Large White Ash Gourd Halwa)

Kacchi-Keri-No-Murambo 25
(Raw Mango Marmalade)

Bafela Safarchan (Stewed Apples) 25

Dudh-Ni-Sev (Vermicelli Cooked In Milk) 25

Badam Na Makrum (Almond Macaroons) 26

Nariel Na Makrum (Coconut Macaroons) 26

Badam Paak (Almond Halwa) 27

Kopra Paak (Coconut Sweet) 27

Mittha Toast (French Toast) 28

Bhakras (Sweet Fried Cookies) 28

Badam-Ne-Pista-Ni-Chikki 29
(Almond and Pista Toffee)

Mumra-Ni-Chikki (Puffed Rice Toffee) 29

Karkaria (Banana Fritters) 29

Mawa Na Paancake 30
(Mawa Pancakes)

Mathura Na Penda (Penda) 30

Popatjee (An unusual Parsi Sweet
Dunked in Sugar Syrup) 31

Chokha Na Ata Noo Aaoud 31

(Rice Flour Sweet)

Gor Papri — No. 1 (A Jaggery Sweet) 32

Gor Papri — No. 2 (Sweet Jaggery Diamonds) 32

Dar Ni Pori 33

Kerana Pattice Athwa Kervai 34

(Banana Pattice Stuffed with Dry Fruits)

Mango Milk Shake 34

Khajoor Ni Ghari (Date Pastry) 35

Cold Milk 35

Minocheher and Tehmi Behram – Kamdin's
Method For Varadhvara 36

(Delicious Fried Wheat Cakes)

Varadhvara 37

Fish

A Visit to the Docks and Fort Fish Market 38

Papeta-ne-Macchi-na-Cutles 38

(Potato Fish Cakes)

Macchi-Na-Cutles (Fish Cutlets) 39

Lal Masala Bharela Bangra 39

(Red Chutney Stuffed Mackerel)

Govarsing-Ne-Gharab No-Patio 40

(Sweet and Sour Cluster Beans cooked with Bhing
Fish Roe — A Traditional Favourite from Gujarat

Lili Chutney Bharela Chhamna 41

(Pomfret Stuffed With Green Chutney)

Karachla-Ni-Kari (Crab Curry) 41

Sookka Boomla No Tarapori Patio 42

(Dried Bombay Duck Pickle)

Tarela Taja Boomla 42

[Fresh Bombay Ducks Fried (First Method)]

Tarela Taja Boomla 43

[Fresh Bombay Ducks Fried (Second Method)]

Maiji No Taja Boomla No Ras (My Great
Grandmother's Fresh Bombay Duck Gravy) 43

Valsad No Lodhi Per No Sukka
Boomla No Patio 44

(Valsad type Dried Bombay Ducks cooked
on a Griddle)

Dehnu No Lévti-No-Patio 44

(Patia of Mud-Fish)

Kesar-Ma-Ramas-Na-Tukra 45

(Salmon Fillets Cooked in Saffron Sauce)

Soonamai-Ni–Tareli Sondh 45

(Soonamai's Fried Lobsters)

Macchi–Ni–Kari 46

(Special Prawn or Fish Currry)

Tareli Macchi (Fried Fish Parsi style) 46

Bapaiji No Kolmi-No-Patio 47

(Grandmother's Prawn Patio)

Piroja's Khatti-Mitthi-Boi 47

(Piroja's Mullets In Hot Sour Gravy)

Kolmi-Na-Kabab (Prawn Kababs) 48

Sasuji No Ambar-No-Lodhi-Per-No-Patio 48

(Mother-in-law's Shrimps cooked on an
Iron Skillet)

Venghna-Ma-Ambar 49

(Shrimps cooked With Brinjals)

Soonamai-Ni-Malai-Ma Kolmi 49

(Soonamai's Prawns)

Soonamai-Ni-Kolmi-Ne-Papeta-No-Vaghar 50

(Soonamai's Prawn and Potato Salnu)

Kolmi-Na-Bhajia 50

(Prawn Bhajias or Batter Fried Prawns)

Soonamai-No-Kolmi-Ne-Kera-Ni-Chaal-No-Ras ... 51

(Soonamai's Prawn and Banana Skin Curry)

Kolmi-Ne-Kothmir-Ma-Paneer 51

(Casserole of Prawns and Cottage Cheese)

Kolmi-Ne-Lal Kohra-No-Saak 52

(Red Pumpkin and Prawn Casserole)

Masala-Ni-Kolmi 52

(Prawns Cooked in Hot Gravy)

Soonamai Na Bhida-Ma-Kolmi 53

(Lady-fingers Cooked with Prawns)

Kacchi-Keri-Ambar-Ma-Randheli 53

(Raw Mangoes Cooked with Baby Shrimps)

Cheese Lagarela Fillet Tamota Na
Sauce Sathe 54

(Crumb Fried Cheese Fish Fillets with Hot
tomato sauce)

Tareli Kolmi 54

(Parsi Fried Prawns)

Macchi Na Fillet Tartare Sauce Ni Sathe 55
(Frilled Fillets with Tartare Sauce)
Party Recipe (Fish Au Gratin) 56

Chicken
Kaju-Ni-Marghi (Boneless Chicken
cooked in Cashew Nut Gravy) 57
Freny-Ni-Makhan-Ma-Randheli-Aakhi-Marghi
(Roast Chicken Freny Style) 58
Aleti-Paleti (Chicken Liver Gravy With Gizzards) 59
Lila-Mari-Ni-Kesari-Marghi 59
(Green Pepper Chicken In Saffron Sauce)
Masala-Pechdar-Marghi 60
(Tasty Chicken Masala)
Marghi-No-Khurmo 60
(Chicken Khurma)
Dilkhush Marghi 61
(Chicken Delight)
Khushbudar Marghi 62
(Fragrant Poppy and Cashew Chicken)

Eggs
Parsi Pora (Omelette) 62
Parsi Poro (Parsi Omelettes) 63
Leeli Keri Ne Vengnani Akoori 63
(Akoori with Raw Mangoes and Brinjal)
Akoori 64
Sooka Boomla Ni Akoori 64
(Akoori with Dried Bombay Ducks)
Boti Ni Akoori 65
(Akoori with finely cut Mutton)
Paneer Charvela Eda Sathe (Scrambled Eggs
with Paneer) 65
Tarkari-Per-Eda 66
(Eggs on Mixed Vegetables)
Ghee Tooria Per Eda 66
(Eggs on Smooth Skinned Gourd)
Sali Per Eda (Chicken in a Haystack) 67
Bafela Eda Ni Curry (Boiled Egg Curry) 67
Kera Per Eda (Eggs on Fried Bananas) 68
Bhida-Per-Eda (Eggs on Lady Fingers) 68
Eda Chutney Na Pattice 69
Egg and Chutney Pattice

Kolmi Bharelo Poro 69
(Prawn Stuffed Omelettes)

Of Brains, Livers and Mutton
Bheja-Na-Cutles (Brain Cutlets) 70
Tamota-Ma-Bhejoo 71
(Brains Cooked with Tomatoes)
Lasan-Ne-Kothmir-Nu-Bhejoo 71
(Brains with Fresh Garlic and Coriander)
Bhunjeli Kaleji (Skewered Roasted
Goats Liver) 72
Papeto-Kaleji (Masala Potato Liver) 72
Kharoo Gos (Basic Mutton Gravy) 73
Bapaiji No Gos-No-Ras 73
(Grandma's Mutton Ras or Gravy)
Mamma No Bafaat (Mothers
Mutton Bafaat) 74
Soonamai-Ni-Papeti-Kandi-Ma Gos 75
(Soonamai's Baby Onions and Baby Potatoes
in Mutton Gravy)
Gos Malai-Dar (Mutton Cooked with Cream) 75
Bhunjeli-Gos-Ni-Tang 76
(Roast Leg of Lamb)
Masoor-Ma-Gos 76
(Lentils cooked with Mutton)
Saro Mutton Bafaat 77
(Richman's Mutton Bafaat)
Khara-Gos Ma Kamodio-Kand (Mutton
Gravy with Fried Purple Yam) 77
Chora Ma Kharia 78
(Trotters with Black Eyed Beans)
Mutton-No-Bafaat 78
(Savoury Mutton with Boiled Eggs)
Kismis-Khima-Na-Pattice 79
(Raisin and Mince Pattice)
Kesri Kabab Jerdaloo-Na-Ras-Ma 80
(Meatballs in Apricot Gravy)
Khimo-Sali-Vatana-Sathe 81
[Mutton Mince with Green Peas and Potato
Shoestrings (Sali)]
Khimo (Minced Mutton) 81
Special Gos-Na-Cutles 82
(Frilled Mutton Cutlets)

Gos-Na-Cutles 82
(Minced Meat Cutlets)

Tam-Tamta-Gos-Na-Kabab 83
(Hot Mutton Kababs)

Papao-Ni-Gravy-Ma-Cutles 83
(Mutton Cutlets in Papaya Gravy)

Maiji Na Lach-Lach Ta Kaju Ma Kofta 84
(Delicious Koftas in Kaju Gravy)

Masala-Na-Chaap 85
(Savoury Mutton Chops)

Dodhi-Ya-Kakri-Ni-Buriyani 85
(White Gourd Or Large Cucumbers Cooked
in Mutton Gravy)

Badami Curry (Almond Curry) 86

Gos-Ni-Kari (Mutton Curry) 86

Aimai No Leelo Ras 87
(Aimai's Green Nergisi Kofta Curry)

Rice

Sado Gos-No-Pulao 88
(Simple Mutton Pulao)

Badshahi Kesri Pulao 89
(Emperor's Mutton Pulao)

Dumbo-Marghi-Pulao Bharelo (Lamb
Stuffed with Chicken Pulao and Roasted) 90

Soonamai-No-Keri-No Pulao 90
(Soonamai's Mango Pulao)

Lehzat Wallo Pulao 91
(Delicious Aromatic Pulao)

Kheema Malai Pulao 92
(Mince Pulao with Cream)

Mamma No Simla Marcha
Bharelo Pulao 93
(Mamma's Stuffed Capsicum Pulao)

Freny-No-Kofta-No-Pulao 94
(Freny's Meatball Pulao)

Nargolio-Kolmi-No-Pulao 95
(Delicious Prawn Pulao from Nargol)

Tatreli Marghi-No-Pulao 96
(Savoury Chicken Pulao)

Macchi-Ne-Tambota-No Pulao 97
(Fish Pulao with Tomatoes)

Vegetarian Food

Patrel (Colocasia Savoury Rolls) 99

Surti-Papri-Nu-Undhioo 100
(Surti Bean Casserole)

Papri (Broad Bean Vegetable) 101

Lagan-Sara-Istew (Vegetable Stew) 102

Galka Ya Ghee Tooria Ni Tarkari 102
(Cooked Sponge Gourd)

Tarkari Ni Kari (Vegetable Curry) 103

Chaas Payelo Sakarkand 103
(Caramelised Sweet Potatoes)

Nariel Na Dudh Ma Randhelu Cauliflower 104
(Cauliflower Cooked in Coconut Milk)

Sambhariya Bheeda 104
(Lady Fingers Cooked In Sambar Masala)

The Ubiquitous Brinjal 105

Jeena Vengna Paneer Sathe Bhunjela 105
(Baked Baby Brinjals)

Vaghareli Faraj Beej 106
(Sauteed Frenchbeans)

Chana Ni Dar Ma Dodhi 106
(White Gourd Cooked in Chana Dal)

Vengna-Na-Bhajiya (Brinjal Bhajias) 107

Vengna-Na-Cutles (Brinjal Fritters) 107

Ravaiya (Chutney Stuffed Brinjals) 108

Vengna Ne Simla Mirchi Nu Salnoo 108
(Bringal Capsicum Salan)

Kaccha Tambota Ma Vengna 109
(Brinjals Cooked with Raw Tomatoes)

Vengna Nu Bharat 109
(Brinjals Cooked with Yoghurt)

Papeta Na Sada Pattice (Potato Cakes) 110

Khaman Pattice (Potato Balls Stuffed
with freshly grated Coconut) 110

Kaccha Tamotama Double Beej 111
(Double Beans Cooked in Raw Tomatoes)

Sekta Ni Sing Ma Toovar Dar 111
(Masala Dal with Drumsticks)

Chora (Black Eyed Beans) 112

Lal Rajma Ni Dar (Rajma Dal) 112

Tittori (Sprouted Bitter Beans) 113

Masoor 113

Keri Nakheli Chana Ni Dar 114
(Chana Dal with Raw Mangoes)
Toovar Ni Dar (Pigeon Peas) 114
Sunna-Na-Dana-No-Pulao 115
(Golden Beads Toovar Dal Pulao)
Mung Ni Dal Ne Papeta 116
(Moong Dal with Potatoes)
Tarkari Ni Khichdi 116
(Rich Vegetable Khichdi)
Meva Ne Tarkari No Pulao 117
(Dried Fruit And Vegetable Pulao)
Kaju Saathe Khichdi Pulao 118
(Luscious Khichdi Pulao)
Dhansakh Na Vagharela Chaval 118
(Dhansakh Whole Spice Rice)

Breads
Chokha Ni Rotli (Rice Flour Rotlis) 119
Kesar Ni Rotli (Saffron Rotlis) 119
Papeta – Na – Paratha (Potato Bread) 120
Mitthi Puri (Sweet Puris) 120

Pickles Preserves etc.
Bufenu (Ripe Mango Pickle in Oil) 121
Keri-Nu-Pani-Nu-Achaar 122
(Mango Pickle in Brine)
Pani-Nu-Karvanda-Nu-Achaar 122
(Karvanda Pickle in Brine)
Limbu-Marcha-Nu-Achaar 123
(Lemon and Chilli Pickle in Oil)
Piroja Nu Vengnanu Achaar 123
(Mother's Brinjal Pickle)
Bhing Ni Gharub Nu Achaar 124
(Bhing Fish Roe Pickle)
Chammna Nu Achaar (Pomfret Pickle) ... 124
Kolmi-Kanda-Tamota Nu Achaar 125
(Prawn, Onion and Tomato Pickle)
Kolmi Nu Khattu-Mitthu Achaar 125
(Sweet and Sour Prawn Pickle)
Pachrasiya Achaar No. 1 126
(Mixed Vegetable Pickle)
Pachrasiya Achaar No. 2 126
(Mixed Vegetable Pickle)

Keri Mewa Nu Achaar 127
(Raw Mango and Dried Fruit Pickle)
Methioo 128
(Mango And Fenugreek Pickle in Oil)
Mrs. Deboo Nu Methianoo Achaar 128
(Mrs. Deboo's Methianoo Pickle)
Chundo (No. 1) (Grated Mango Chutney) ... 129
Chundo (No. 2) (Grated Mango Chutney) ... 129
Koprana Dudh Ni Kachumber 129
(Coconut Milk Salad)
Bapaiji Ni Tamota Ni Chutney 130
(Grandma's Tomato Chutney)
Nariel Ni Chutney 130
(Green Coconut Chutney)
Keri Ni Chutney (Mango Chutney) 130
Aamli Ni Chutney (Tamarind Chutney) 131
Sareea (Sago Pappads) 131
Cooverbai's Parsi Dhansakh Masala 132
(Parsi Dhansakh Masala)
Adu-Lasan (Ginger, Garlic Paste) 132
Garam Masala 1. (For Rice) 132
Garam Masala 2. (For Mutton, Chicken and
Vegetables) 132

THE PARSI LAGAN-NU-BHONU

The Parsi Wedding Feast

"JAMVA CHALOJI" The lusty booming call from the caterer to the guests at a Parsi Wedding, to partake of the freshly cooked, hot, fragrant dinner that awaits them!

The wedding ceremony takes place on a stage bedecked with flowers at any of the Parsi venues called "Wadis". The guests, after having wished happiness to the couple, wend their way to the bar for cold drinks, while the band plays lively music.

The dinner tables are laid out in long rows covered with white cloth and chairs placed on only one side of the table. Two banana leaves are laid in front of each guest, with a fork and spoon, and a white serviette rolled in a glass. A butler comes with a bowl of ice and places chunks in each glass, followed by the man who pours out a soft drink of your choice. The "rotliwalla" places two thin chapatis on the banana leaf and the "acharwalla" brings a sweet and sour carrot pickle studded with dates and raisins. Next comes a bearer carrying a round thala full of large pieces of pomfret fish doused with a white sweet and sour sauce, topped by cherry tomatoes, freshly chopped coriander and fried onion slices. The fish is followed by deep fried chicken farchas. This may be followed by little baskets or "topli paneers" or a diamond shaped piece of "lagan custard", sweet and creamy with almond slices. Optional dishes are eggs on coriander and tomatoes, or "kid gos", a tender piece of mutton with a large fried potato-half served in white coconut gravy. This is followed by mutton pulao and thick masala dal and finally ice-cream for dessert.

Nowadays, for elaborate functions where a couple of thousand guests are invited, it is the style to lay out buffets, and I have introduced new items such as Chicken and Cheese Salads, Tandoori Murghi, Pahari Murghi, Kaju Mutton, Nargisi Kofta Curry, Rainbow Rice, Chinese Fried Rice, Kheema Malai Pulao, winding up with any one of a variety of ice creams - Banana and Chocolate Chips, Peach Melba, Choco-nut or Rum and Raisin.

I have included in this book all the major items of traditional Wedding dinner. Now for the lunch it is always "Sev" or Sweet Vermicelli with Raisins, Charoli and Almond slices, Sweet "Dahi" in small individual glasses, Sali Boti, White Rice, Yellow Dal and Pomfret Patio.

Two of our fish items which have become famous at Navjote and Wedding banquets are our Fish Fillets with Tartar Sauce and Fish Vindaloo which is a deep red gravy, sweet, sour and hot, sprinkled with green jewel-like pieces of capsicum.

So, open this book and enjoy our Lagan-nu-Bhonu in your very home, to the lusty booming call "JAMVA CHALOJI".

INTRODUCTION

It has been my experience that good cooks are born. At the same time, even an uninspired person who is totally ignorant of kitchenlore, if sufficiently motivated, can learn how to produce good wholesome meals. So people who can't wield magic with their spoons should not be worried. The desire to produce for one's family is a powerful inspiration and will move mountains.

My daughter Freny used to stand on a stool and insist on cooking on her own, with help of course, by the time she was six or seven. She would ask questions and I tried to answer them all. It's very important for a child, girl or boy to know what's cooking in the kitchen, how to cook it and why a particular item is being cooked on a certain day. Having your children around you in the kitchen, will create a pleasant atmosphere of wellbeing, sharing and concern. What you do and say will influence your children subconsciously. My eldest son Kurush could cook a very decent meal by the time he left home to go to college in Poona where he studied for his M.A. degree in Archaeology.

Prime the children's interest in what to buy in the market and how to clean and cook it. My daughter a very enthusiastic young cook, used to leave the kitchen in a mess, to be cleaned up by the servants. I told her that if she wanted to cook — she had to clean up too.

Don't do everything the cook book tells you. If your fancy is caught by some exotic recipe, read it over twice. See what ingredients your family is used to and add chilli powder, chillies, salt, sugar and oil according to YOUR PERSONAL taste. If you are making something new for the first time, taste it before bringing it to the table. Once when we were in Lonavla, Freny made a chocolate mousse. She followed the recipe faithfully and the souffle looked yummy until it was eaten. It barely had any sugar taste and had to be thrown out. What the writer of the cook book says may not be your idea of taste and fun. Always taste a new item before bringing it to the table.

I come from a family of good cooks. Grandmother Cooverbai, was an excellent cook as were her daughters, Khorshed and Hilla, her daughter-in-law Piroja, my mother, also turned out to be a superb cook. Seeing all these ladies in the kitchen and being encouraged by my grandmother, I am today a caterer who can furnish meals for a couple of thousand people at a time.

There are some memories of childhood that we sometimes cannot shake off. My parents, myself and my two brothers lived in a lovely old bungalow in Bandra. My mothers family of maternal great-grandparents, an aunt and several uncles lived in a small village called Tadgaon, on the coast of Gujarat.

During May vacation, my mother, myself and my brother Meherji went for a month's holiday to Gujarat where we were loved beyond reason by our great-grandfather. For the whole of this month we ran around the wild young things eating the skinny dates or khajurs which grew in profusion on the date palms, and innumerable types of boras and mangoes and invariably came home to Bombay laden with boils, fever, cuts and bruises. But this one month in the year, we were foot loose and fancy free and roamed in the dry dust wherever we wanted.

The grandparents lived in a mud and dung plastered house, built with bamboos and wood and thatched in certain parts with terracotta tiles. As soon as the huge gate made of wood and covered with thorn branches called "jhanpo" was pushed aside, the first thing that came into view was the kitchen with its wooden barred window with smoke trailing up from it and the verandah with the dining table and four wooden chairs.

Now after 40 years I wonder how great grandmother Soonamai managed her big household and fed so many servants and their entire families, about 40 of them, month after month and year after year. She and great-grandfather both died when I was 14 and in college. I remember rushing off to Nargol too late to say goodbye. I never went there, ever again. But the memories of delicious golden fried eggs with crinkly whites at the edges is in front of my eyes, to this day. The old lady was a wonderful cook and was in the habit of grinding fresh turmeric for her kababs and curries. She taught me by her example, how to makeshift and do without certain spices, how to substitute one masala for another.

I learned my lessons of thrift and perseverance from Soonamai and Cooverbai, and I owe to them for my success and prosperity.

HISTORICAL BACKGROUND OF THE PARSIS

The Parsis fled their "mader vatan" or mother land after the downfall of the Sassanian Empire in Iran. They settled on the west coast of India because they had knowledge of it through trade and travellers' accounts, but it was as refugees that they landed at Sanjan. From this place they slowly made their way to Navsari, Bharuch, Surat and Kalyan.

Mainly, they were sturdy farmers, and deeply religious. Their forefathers had left everything behind for the sake of their religion and the ones who survived after them were grateful and remembered them in their prayers. It is from these prayer lists —DISAPOTHI — that we get some historical information. The holy fire which the Parsis had brought with them was installed at Udvada in a fire temple which was called an Atash Behram. It is very difficult to install these holy venues as the fire has to be got from 18 different places. Such an Atash Behram has also been installed at Navsari. Here, in 1555, Akbar, the Great Moghul, after his conquest of Surat sent for the learned and pious "Dastur" or priest Meherji-Rana. He was so impressed by this saintly man that he asked him to come to Delhi and learnt many tenets of the Zoroastrian religion which he included in his daily life and in his new religion, the Din-e-Ilahi.

After the advent of the British, Parsi fortunes began to rise. The Parsi was known as an "honest man" and positions of trust soon came his way. All major jobs which included handling of cash or treasuries were in Parsi hands. This position of trust was carried down till the period of Indian Independence in 1947 when most banks had Parsi cashiers.

During the pre-Independence movements, giants like Dadabhoy Naoroji, Madame Bhicaiji Cama and Sir Pherozeshah Mehta rose to back an India for the Indians and freedom from the British Raj. Today, the Parsis are a small community, slowly becoming extinct. The community's death rate is higher than its birth rate and it is anybody's guess how long it will survive.

ROTLI

Preparation Time: 35 mins.
Cooking Time: 35-45 mins.

3   cups wheat flour
$1/_2$ cup ghee or oil
     salt to taste.

1. Place the flour on your work surface. Make a hole in the centre and pour in the ghee. Add the salt and mix with your fingertips. Add a cup of water in a trickle and knead with both your hands till soft and smooth. Keep in a cool place for half an hour.

2. Make small even sized balls out of the dough. Place a skillet or tava on the fire. Roll out each ball neatly into a thin round as big as a saucer. Place on the hot skillet and turn over three to four times till cooked. Do not use any oil on top to help cook the rotlis.

GAJAR-MEWA-NU-ACHAAR

(Carrot and Dried Fruit Pickle)

Preparation Time: Overnight
Cooking Time: 40 mins.

4   cups grated carrots
3-4 cups sugar
1   teaspoon garam masala
$1/_2$ teaspoon cardamom and nutmeg powder
3   tablespoons chilli powder
1   tablespoon turmeric powder
     sugarcane vinegar as necessary
$1/_2$ cup raisins — seedless ⎫ soak in
$1/_2$ cup dried apricots   ⎬ vinegar
$1/_2$ cup dried dates kharak ⎭ overnight
2   tablespoons finely sliced, dried garlic
     salt to taste

1. Place the grated carrots in a heavy based pan. Add three to four cups of sugar and two to three cups of vinegar and cook over a slow fire. Keep stirring. Add the garlic.

2. If you need more vinegar to soften the carrots use it — a little at a time. When the carrots are soft, toss in the soaked dried fruit and bring to a boil. When the sauce thickens add the powdered spices. Stir the mixture well. Taste for sugar as well as salt. The pickle should be more sweet than sour. Remove from heat and cool.

3. Fill in clean glass bottles.

MACCHI-NO-SAHAS

([Method 1] Fish Sauce – with Rice Flour).

Preparation Time: 15-20 mins.
Cooking Time: 30-35 mins. • Serves: 6-8.

2 pomfrets – sliced into 8 to 10 pieces
2 onions – sliced and deep fried
2 onions finely chopped
10 cherry tomatoes
18 green chillies deseeded and finely chopped
2 tablespoons cumin seeds ⎫ finely
2 pods garlic ⎬ ground
1/2 bunch fresh coriander ⎭
3 eggs
1/2 cup sugarcane vinegar
1/2 cup sugar
1 cup rice flour
   oil

1. Take a large mouthed dekchi and cook two large chopped onions in one cup oil. When they become soft and pink add the ground garlic, cumin and the rice flour. Lower the flame and stir the mixture back and forth till well roasted. Add three to four cups of water and whisk briskly so that there are no flour granules and the liquid is well blended with the flour. Allow to cook on a medium flame and keep stirring non-stop till the liquid thickens.

2. Wash and salt the pomfret slices and when the liquid bubbles add the fish, cherry tomatoes, and the green chillies. Lower the heat and allow the fish to cook till soft.

3. Take the eggs and whisk them well in a bowl. Add the sugar and vinegar to the beaten eggs and mix well.

4. When the fish is cooked, slowly pour the above mixture in a thin dribble onto the fish gravy and shake the pan vigorously from side to side. Remove from heat after tasting for salt.

5. Deep fry two sliced onions till crisp and brown.

6. Serve the fish sauce on a flat dish and cover with finely chopped fresh coriander and the crisply fried onions.

MACCHI-NO-SAHAS

([Method 2] Fish Sauce – with Gram Flour)

Preparation Time: 15-20 mins.
Cooking Time: 30-35 mins. • Serves: 6-8

2 pomfrets sliced into 8 to 10 pieces
2 onions – sliced finely and deep fried
2 onions – finely chopped
4 large tomatoes, skinned and finely chopped
1/2 bunch fresh coriander
1 tablespoon Kashmiri chilli powder
2 pods garlic
2 tablespoons cumin seeds ⎫ To be finely
18 deseeded green chillies ⎬ ground in a little water
2 eggs ⎭
1/2 cup sugarcane vinegar
1/2 cup sugar
1 cup gram flour
   salt
   oil

1. Cook the two chopped onions in a wide mouthed vessel, along with one cup oil. When the onion becomes soft add the ground masala and fry it well. Then add one cup gram flour and chilli powder and stir well. If necessary add a little extra oil. When the flour becomes a smooth paste add three to four cups water and the chopped tomatoes and stir non-stop till you have a smooth thick gravy.

2. Wash the fish slices well. Salt them When the gravy boils and begins to thicken, drop in the fish slices and allow to cook till soft on a low flame. Remove from the flame.

3. Stir the sugar and vinegar together and add the two beaten eggs to it. Mix well till the sugar has dissolved and add to the fish gravy in a slow trickle, stirring the sauce carefully to ensure that the fish is not broken nor the gravy, turned into scrambled eggs because of the heat of the sauce. Cover with fried onions and the freshly chopped coriander just before serving.

4. Some people prefer the white type of sauce whilst some prefer this slightly red one. Both taste good. You can substitute rawas slices or prawns for the pomfret slices.

5. This sauce is invariably served at birthday, navjote and wedding celebrations.

6. It can be made with boiled, salted meat instead of fish. Use one kilo to one and a half kilo meat for the amounts given in the recipe. The soup should be strained and used instead of water.

MARGHI-NA-FARCHA

(Fried Chicken)

Preparation Time: 30-35 mins.
Cooking Time: 15 mins. • Serves: 4-6

8   pieces of chicken
$1\frac{1}{2}$ teaspoons ginger-garlic paste
$1\frac{1}{2}$ teaspoons Kashmiri chilli powder
$\frac{3}{4}$ teaspoon turmeric powder
$1\frac{1}{2}$ teaspoons cinnamon, clove and black pepper powder
2   green chillies
1   tablespoon coriander
$\frac{1}{2}$ stalk celery
1   cup bread crumbs
3-4 eggs
    salt
    oil for frying.

1. Wash the chicken and marinate it with salt and ginger-garlic paste. Coat it with the chilli, turmeric and 3 spice powders. Allow to stand for half an hour. Place the chicken in a heavy bottomed pan along with the chillies, celery, coriander and one cup of water. Place over a low fire and allow to simmer till the flesh is soft and tender. Remove from fire.

2. Coat the chicken pieces with the bread crumbs.

3. Place oil in a kadhai on high heat. Beat 3-4 eggs. Dip the chicken pieces in the beaten eggs two or three at a time and fry in hot oil till golden brown. Serve with potato chips and a green salad.

LAGAN-NA-TARKARI-PER-EDA

(Wedding style Eggs on Tomatoes and Coriander)

Preparation Time: 15 mins.
Cooking Time: 20-30 mins. • Serves: 12.

16   eggs
4   onions sliced and deep fried
6   large tomatoes, skinned and deseeded
4   green chillies deseeded and finely chopped
1   bunch coriander cleaned, washed, finely chopped
1½   tablespoons sugarcane vinegar
2   tablespoons sugar
1   teaspoon red chilli powder
1   teaspoon garam masala powder
1   teaspoon ginger-garlic paste
     salt
3   tablespoons ghee

1. Take a large heavy bottomed thali. Place the ghee and ginger-garlic paste in it and place over medium heat. Stir for two minutes and add the green chillies, chopped tomatoes, coriander, vinegar, sugar, chilli powder and garam masala and cook till the tomatoes are soft. Sprinkle fine salt and the sliced onions over the tomato mixture and mix well. Flatten the mixture evenly in the thali and make sixteen depressions in the mixture. Lower heat.

2. Break each egg separately in a saucer and slip it on the mixture so that the yolks fall into the depressions. Sprinkle lightly with fine salt. Cover and cook. Do not allow eggs to become hard.

LAGAN-NU-CUSTARD

(Wedding Custard)

Preparation Time: 40 mins.
Cooking Time: 40-50 mins. • Serves: 12-15.

10   eggs
3   litres full cream milk
½   tin condensed milk
600   gms. sugar
15   boiled and sliced almonds
50   gms. boiled and sliced pistachios
½   teaspoon powdered nutmeg and cardamom
1½   teaspoons vanilla essence
      butter for greasing the dish

1. Bring the milk to a boil in a large heavy bottomed pan. Remove from the fire and stir in the condensed milk, sugar and cook over a slow fire. Taste the milk and add another half cup of sugar only if necessary. Keep stirring the milk till it is sticky and ivory in colour. Remove from the fire and cool.

2. Grease a pyrex dish or two small ones with butter.

3. Beat the eggs till frothy and stir into the cooled milk. Beat in the vanilla and nutmeg-cardamom powder. Pour into the pyrex dishes and bake in the oven at 350°F till golden brown.

4. Remove from the oven, top with the sliced nuts and pop it back into the oven and switch off.

5. Chill and serve, preferably the next day.

KERI-NU-ICECREAM

(Mango Ice-cream)

Preparation Time: 15 mins. • Chilling Time: 10 mins. It depends on how long it takes to turn hard

The pulp of 16 Alphonso mangoes or
2 packets Mafco mango pulp
1½ litres fresh milk
1 kg. sugar
2 tins condensed milk
1 pinch baking powder
16 eggs – optional
a little pinch saffron colouring
10-15 kg. ice
2 kg. black salt
a 5 litre ice-cream mould

1. Boil the milk with sugar for ten minutes. Add the mango pulp, whisked eggs, colour and the condensed milk and stir vigorously. Add baking powder last. Mix once again.

2. Pack the hand mould with crushed ice and black salt after placing the empty ice-cream container carefully in the churn. Pour the mixture in the metal container and seal carefully.

3. Then keep turning the churn handle till the ice-cream gets cold and hard and will not turn anymore. Pack more ice into the churn and cover with a thick gunny bag. The ice-cream will remain firm in the churn for about an hour.

4. Serve it in the mango season in long stemmed glasses topped with bits of ripe mango.

MALAI-NA-PARATHA

(Malai Parathas)

Preparation Time: 45 mins.
Cooking Time: 45 mins. • Makes: 12

300 gms. wheat flour
50 gms. thick malai or cream
water or milk
salt
pure ghee

1. Place the seived flour on your work surface and make a hole in the centre. Add in the cream, salt to taste and half a cup of water or milk and mix with your fingers. Knead the dough with enough water till it becomes soft and smooth. Place in a covered bowl for half an hour.

2. Divide the mixture into twelve round balls and cover with a damp cloth. Take one ball at a time and roll it into a large circle. Apply ghee. Carefully fold both opposite flaps into the centre of the circle and then fold again from the sides till you get a small square packet. Roll out into a square paratha.

3. Place on a hot griddle and turn the side. Add half a teaspoon of ghee and turn. Add another teaspoon of ghee till both sides are golden-brown in colour. Turn sides again and place in a warm dish. Finish all the parathas in the same manner.

GOS-NO-PULAO

(Mutton Pulao)

Preparation Time: 30 mins. • Cooking Time with use of Pressure Cooker: 1 hr. • Serves: 15-18.

$1\frac{1}{2}$ kgs. basmati rice
2 kgs. mutton
2 tablespoons ginger-garlic paste
1 kg. potatoes
$\frac{1}{4}$ teaspoon jelabi colour
Grind together in your mixer:
10 Kashmiri chillies
20 black peppercorns
1 small packet saffron
1 teaspoon javantri or mace
2 badian or star anise
1 teaspoon shahjeera or carraway seeds — grind together
4 cloves
1" stick cinnamon
$\frac{1}{2}$ nutmeg
2 black large elchas
1 cup curd
2 large onions – finely chopped
2 large onions – finely sliced
4 large tomatoes
4 bay leaves or tamal patta
$\frac{1}{2}$ cup raisins
1 cup fried whole cashewnuts
6 boiled eggs cut into quarters
salt to taste
ghee

1. Divide the rice into two portions. Boil one half with a pinch of Jelabi colour and 2 bay leaves in salted water. Drain the rice and set aside.

   Cook the other half in salted water with 2 bay leaves and when soft, drain and set aside.

2. Grind all the spices finely. Marinate the washed mutton pieces in ginger-garlic paste, curds and salt for 10 minutes.

3. Deep fry the sliced onions. Skin and cube the potatoes. Salt them and deep fry them till soft. Set aside.

4. Place the chopped onions along with $1\frac{1}{2}$ cups of ghee in which the onions and potatoes were fried. Cook until light brown and then add the ground spices. Stir for 2 minutes and add the mutton pieces. Cook for 5-7 minutes in the masala and then add 4-5 cups of water and cook in a pressure cooker until soft.

5. Empty the mutton and gravy into a large vessel and burn off the excess liquid until 2 cups of gravy is left.

6. Fry the raisins and cashewnuts. Boil the eggs. Peel and cut vertically into 4 pieces.

7. Layer the pulao with white rice, mutton, potatoes and a final layer of saffron rice. Garnish the top layer with fried onions, cashewnuts, eggs and raisins. Cover tightly with foil, place a lid on the vessel and keep over a low flame for 20 minutes before serving.

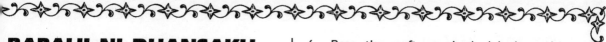

BAPAIJI NI DHANSAKH NI DAR

(Traditional Parsi Dal)

Preparation Time: 25-30 mins.
Cooking Time: 45 mins. • Serves: 8-10.

400 gms. pink masoor dal OR toovar dal
150 gms. red pumpkin
100 gms. brinjal
350 gms. tomatoes
1   bunch spring onions
4   tiny methi bhaji bunches
1   white radish leaves
6   green chillies deseeded
1   teacup chopped coriander
2   sprigs curry leaves
2   teaspoons turmeric powder
1   tablespoon chilli powder to taste
2   tablespoons Parsi dhansakh masala
2   tablespoons sambhar masala
1 1/2 tablespoons ginger-garlic paste
2   raw mangoes
6   drumsticks cut into small pieces
    salt to taste
1   cup pure ghee

1. Clean the drumsticks, cut each into 3 to 4 pieces and boil in salted water. Drain and set aside.

2. Wash the dal and soak it in water for 15-20 minutes.

3. Wash and chop the spring onions, chillies, methi bhaji, brinjal, pumpkin and radish leaves.

4. Wash the dal twice and put into a pressure cooker. Add the washed, chopped vegetables, turmeric and chilli powders and ginger-garlic paste. Add salt to taste. Add 6-7 cups water and cook till soft.

5. Wash the tomatoes and chop them finely and place them in a large dekchi along with one cup ghee and curry leaves. Cook over a slow fire.

6. Pass the soft, cooked dal through a moulee legume or mixie.

7. When the tomatoes soften, add the sambar and dhansakh masalas and two skinned chopped green mangoes if you like. When the masala has cooked, add the pureed dal and allow to simmer for 15 minutes. Add the boiled drumsticks and serve with brown fried rice, kababs and kachumber or plain mutton pulao.

DODHI–NO–MURAMBO

(White Pumpkin Halwa)

Preparation Time: 20 mins.
Cooking Time: 1 hr. 40 mins. • Serves: 10-12.

1/2 kg. white pumpkin, grated
500 gms. sugar
1   kg. cream
1   teaspoon green cardamom seeds
1/2 cup rose water
    silver leaves or vark

1. Squeeze the water from the grated dodhi and set aside. Take a heavy vessel and boil the dodhi in the squeezed water for 40 minutes. Add the sugar and lower the flame and allow to simmer for half an hour. Add the cardamom seeds and allow to simmer for another 15 minutes. If the dodhi is soft and tender when tasted, stir the cream into the mixture and remove from the fire after 10 minutes. Add the rose water.

2. Place in a dish and cover with silver leaves or vark.

SALI-NE-JARDALOO-MA-GOS

(Sweet and sour mutton gravy with apricots and potato shoestrings)

Preparation Time: 20 mins. • Cooking Time on Gas Stove: 2½-3 hrs. • Serves: 8-10

1	kg. mutton boti or tiny pieces of mutton with nali
5	large onions finely chopped
20	dried apricots, washed and soaked overnight in a jar containing quarter cup vinegar, half cup water and half cup sugar
400	gms. sali or potato shoestrings
2	tablespoons powdered garam masala
1	teaspoon chilli powder
½	teaspoon turmeric powder
½	teaspoon black pepper powder
3	tablespoons raisins ⎫ ground in a
3	tablespoons cashewnuts ⎬ little water
1	tablespoon ginger-garlic paste
1	two-inch square piece of dried kopra finely ground in a little water
2	cups chopped tomatoes
	coriander leaves for garnishing
	salt
	oil

1. Place half cup oil and the onions to cook in a heavy bottomed pan. When golden coloured, and the salted washed mutton botis, ginger-garlic paste and fry the mutton till red. Gradually add the powdered masalas, tomatoes and ground dried kopra and cook on a low heat for 10 minutes.

2. Pour one litre water and allow to cook till tender. This will take two to three hours on a gas fire. Keep adding water till the meat is tender.

3. Pressure cooked mutton is always tender and less troublesome to deal with, but mutton cooked on a slow coal fire is always more tasty. However great care has to be taken to see that it doesn't burn when cooked on an open fire or gas stove.

4. When the meat is cooked, drop in the ground raisins and cashewnuts and cook for 10 minutes. Add the apricots soaked overnight along with the vinegar and sugar liquid. Cover the pan, cook for 5 minutes and remove from the fire.

5. Serve on a flat dish and sprinkle lavishly with sali and decorate with bunches of coriander leaves.

6. On festive occasions, mostly birthdays, top the sali with half cup broken cashew nuts, deep fried, along with the chopped coriander.

LAGAN-NU-ACHAAR

(Wedding Pickle)

Preparation Time: 45 mins. – 1 hr.
Cooking Time: 35-45 mins.

2	kgs. grated carrots
300	gms. seedless raisins
300	gms. dried apricots
300	gms. dried dates chopped finely
50	gms. sliced, dried ginger, cut julienne
50	gms. cherry sized round red dried chillies
100	gms. sliced dried garlic
100	gms. dried boras
2	kgs. sugar
1/4	kg. jaggery
1 1/2	bottles malt-sugar cane vinegar
2	tablespoons chilli powder
2	tablespoons black pepper, cinnamon, cloves, nutmeg and cardamom powder
	salt to taste

(raisins and dried apricots) soaked overnight in one cup sugar and as much vinegar as necessary

1. Place the grated carrots, sugar jaggery and one bottle vinegar in a heavy bottomed pan and allow to cook over a slow fire. When soft add the sliced ginger and garlic and salt to taste.

2. When the carrots are cooked and you have a nice sticky syrup add the chopped dates, boras, red chillies, raisins and apricots. Bring the pickle to a slow boil, add the chilli powder and garam masala powder and remove from the fire. Cool and fill into jars.

3. This pickle can be preserved for several years if handled properly and kept in a cool, dark place.

PATRA-NI-MACCHI

(Fish in Banana Leaves)

Preparation Time: 25 mins.
Cooking Time: 15 mins. • Serves: 6-8.

2	large pomfrets, each cut into 5 slices

For the chutney:

1	freshly grated coconut
2	cups freshly chopped coriander
1	tablespoon chopped mint
1"	piece fresh ginger
20	cloves garlic
6	green chillies deseeded
10	peppercorns
1	tablespoon cumin seeds
2	sour limes, juice removed
2	tablespoons sugar
	salt to taste
6	large very soft banana leaves
1/2	cup vinegar
1/2	cup water
1/2	cup oil

(coconut through sour limes) grind finely

1. Wash the pomfrets twice, apply salt and set aside.

2. Grind the chutney masala till it is soft and buttery. Use half a cup of water if necessary.

3. Prepare the banana leaves by removing the centre stalk. You will have twelve pieces now. Take one slice of fish at a time and smother it in the chutney. It should be well coated and then wrap it in one piece of banana leaf into a neat package. Tie with thin white thread. When all the slices are neatly packed take an aluminium tray and grease it with half a cup of oil. Place on a medium flame and arrange the packages on the hot tray. Leave for three minutes, then turn over once. Sprinkle with water and vinegar and cover tightly. Allow to cook over a low flame for 15 minutes, turning over the packages at least once. Serve immediately.

SHIRAZI PULAO

(Saffron, Mutton and Dried Fruit Pulao)

Preparation Time: 30-40 mins.
Cooking Time: 1 hr. • Serves: 8-10

For the Rice
1/2	gm.saffron
1/2	kg. basmati rice
4	bay leaves
2"	piece cinnamon
2	star anise
4	large cardamoms
2	onions finely sliced and deep fried
1/2	cup ghee
1	pinch saffron colour

For the Kababs
200 gms.	minced mutton
2	medium onions finely chopped
8	slices stale bread
1	tablespoon curd
3	raw eggs
1	tablespoon ginger-garlic paste
2	tablespoons fresh coriander chopped
1	tablespoon fresh mint, chopped
4	green chillies, finely chopped
1 1/2	teaspoons black pepper powder
1 1/2	teaspoons fennel powder
	oil for frying

For the Mutton
2	gms. saffron
350 gms.	mutton chunks with nali
1	tablespoon ginger-garlic paste
2	large onions, chopped
100 gms.	dried apricots soaked in water overnight
50 gms.	large, seedless raisins
50 gms.	almonds, boiled, skinned, sliced
1	tablespoon mace, powdered
1/2	teaspoon cinnamon, powdered
1/2	teaspoon cloves, powdered
1"	piece kopra
1/2	cup pure ghee
	salt

{ ground fine in 1 tablespoon of water }

For the decoration
6	eggs, boiled
4	onions, finely sliced, deep fried

1. Cook the rice in two portions. Make one white and the other use saffron colour. Mix half the sliced, fine onions into the cooked rice. If you wish you can boil the rice in water along with the spices and drain it when cooked or cook it in the spices till the water has evaporated.

2. Wash the mutton and allow it to marinate in salt and the ginger-garlic paste.

3. Keep the boiled eggs ready.

4. Take the minced mutton and place it in a large thali. Add finely chopped onions, two tablespoons coriander, mint, finely chopped green chillies, fennel powder, curd, three raw eggs and ginger-garlic paste. Soak the bread in a small basin of water for five minutes. Then squeeze the bread between both your hands and add it to the mince mixture and mix it well with your hands. Taste for salt. Make small sized meat balls after dipping your hands in water. You should get 20-25 kababs out of this mixture. Take a kadhai and half fill it with oil. Place on high heat and when the oil starts smoking, lower the flame and add five to six kababs at a time in the oil. Stir the oil and fry till the kababs are brown. Set aside.

5. In a vessel place two chopped onions along with half a cup ghee. Cook till pink and soft and then add the ground masalas. Stir and when the masala is cooked, toss in the mutton and fry till red. Add water and the saffron and cook in the pressure cooker till tender.

6. Boil and skin the almonds and cut into fine slivers and fry in a little ghee along with the raisins. Set aside.

7. Take a large vessel and grease it with ghee. Then place a layer of white rice a

the bottom. Cover with a layer of mutton gravy and half the kababs, apricots and fried onions. Repeat this till all the mutton, kababs, white and yellow rice are over. The last layer should be of saffron rice. Top the rice with quartered eggs, and the fried raisins and almonds.

8. Cover firmly with a lid and foil and place over a very low heat for half an hour before serving.

9. Serve with dhansakh dal or an onion kachumber.

KESAR-PISTA KULFI

(Saffron-Pistachio Kulfi)

Preparation Time: Nil
Cooking Time: 30-45 mins. • Serves: 10-15.

2   litres milk
400 gms. sugar
200 gms. crushed pistachio
$1/2$ tin condensed milk
2   gms. saffron
8   drops green food colouring
    kulfi moulds

1. Place milk, sugar and condensed milk in a heavy bottomed pan. Place over a medium flame and stir with a wooden spoon till the mixture becomes almost half the original amount. Add the crushed pistachios and remove from heat. Warm the saffron on a tava and crumble into the mixture and place on a low heat for 5 minutes more. Remove from the fire and cool. Pour into the kulfi moulds and freeze, for 3 to 4 hours.

2. If you wish you can place the mixture in an ice-cream mould, pack it in ice, and churn it by hand till the handle does not turn any more.

SALI-MA-MARGHI
(Chicken with potato shoestring)

Preparation Time: 15 mins.
Cooking Time: 45-50 mins. • Serves: 10

450 gms. fine potato shoestrings (sali)
2   chickens each cut into legs and breasts
     (16 pieces)
1   tablespoon ginger-garlic paste
3   large onions finely chopped
4   large tomatoes, skinned deseeded finely
     chopped
4   green chillies deseeded and finely chopped
$1/2$ cup fresh coriander, finely chopped
2   teaspoons chilli powder
2   teaspoons garam masala
3   crushed green cardamoms
1   teaspoon poppy seeds, roasted and ground
4   bay leaves
2   star anise
     salt
$3/4$ cup peanut refined oil

1. Wash the four chicken breasts and four
    leg pieces and cut each into two. You will
    now have 16 pieces of chicken. Wash
    once again, marinate in the ginger-garlic
    paste, add salt to taste and set aside.

2. Place the onions and oil in a strong, thick
    bottomed vessel. Allow the onion to
    soften over a medium flame. Add the bay
    leaves and star anise. When the onions
    turn golden add the green chillies and
    tomatoes and the crushed cardamoms.
    Stir and cook over a low flame till
    tomatoes soften. Then add the chilli
    powder and garam masala. Cook for 4
    minutes add the chicken and the poppy
    seeds. Stir and allow the chicken to cook
    in its own juice for 10 minutes. Cover.
    Add three teacups of water and allow to
    simmer for 20 minutes till tender.

3. Remove onto a flat dish and sprinkle with
    the chopped coriander and potato
    shoestrings.

PARSI SEV
(Sweet Vermicelli)

Preparation Time: 10 mins.
Cooking Time: 15 mins. • Serves: 6.

No Parsi birthday, navjote or wedding is
complete without this delicious sweet which is
always accompanied by sweet dahi.

250 gms. vermicelli or sev
$1^1/2$ cups sugar
1   teaspoon vanilla essence
1   teaspoon nutmeg-cardamom powder
$1/2$ teacup raisins, fried
$1/2$ teacup charoli or sliced almonds – fried
     ghee for frying

1. Break the vermicelli into one and a half
    inch pieces.

2. Place 2 cups ghee in a flat bottomed,
    wide mouthed vessel and slowly fry the
    vermicelli till golden brown. If you cook
    it over a fast flame it will burn up. Do not
    stir it constantly or the vermicelli will
    break up into tiny pieces. Remove from
    the fire.

3. Drain the ghee.

4. Mix the sugar in 2-3 cups of water as per
    taste.

5. Place the vessel with the vermicelli on
    the fire and add a little sugar water at a
    time, stir gently and cook till soft.

    This sounds easy but it is difficult and you
    may not get it right the first time. You
    may get the sev very pulpy in your first
    attempt. The trick is immense patience.

    Add the sugar water a little at a time and
    cover the vessel and cook. Mix in vanilla
    and the spice powder and cook till soft.

6. Place in a pretty dish and top with fried
    raisins, charoli or almond slices.

    Ideal for breakfast or tea.

MITTHOO DAHI

(Sweets Curd)

Preparation Time: Overnight • Serves: 6.

1   litre milk
1/2   cup sugar
1   tablespoon gelatine
1   tablespoon curd
1/2   teaspoon vanilla essence
1/2   teaspoon cardamom-nutmeg powder
       fresh pink rose petals

1. Boil the milk once. Add the sugar and bring to the boil four times and set aside.

2. Melt the gelatine in half a cup of water and add it to the sugared milk. Cool the milk.

3. Dip your finger in the curd and pass it around the bowl in which you are going to set the curd.

4. Mix the remaining curd in a teacup with the vanilla essence and spice powder and mix it into the tepid milk mixture. Pour into the prepared bowl and allow to set overnight. Leave covered in a warm place.

5. Decorate with rose petals and chill before serving the next day.

DHAN-DAR

(White Rice, and Yellow Dal)

Preparation Time: 15 mins.
Cooking Time: 30 mins. • Serves: 6-8

500 gms. toovar dal
1 1/4 teaspoons turmeric powder
2   large onions slice and deep fried
5   green chillies deseeded and finely chopped
1   pod garlic skinned sliced and deep fried
4   tablespoons chopped coriander
       salt to taste
1   cup pure ghee

1. Wash the dal twice. Place in a pressure cooker with six to seven cups of water. Add the necessary amount of salt and turmeric and cook for 15 minutes after the whistle.

2. Deep-fry sliced onion, chopped chillies in ghee. Remove the onions when golden brown. Remove chillies as soon as you put them in the ghee.

3. Pass the dal through a moulé legume. Allow to simmer for five minutes. Add the pure ghee and place dal in a bowl topped with the fried onions, garlic, chillies and coriander.

4. This dal should only be eaten with white rice and a patia. This patia can be made with fish, prawns, eggs or brinjals.

CHAMNA-NE-KOLMI-NO-PATIO

(Prawn and Pomfret Patia)

Preparation Time: 15-20 mins.
Cooking Time: 35-45 mins. • Serves: 6-8

300 gms.	large deveined prawns
10	slices pomfret fish
2	large onions chopped
4	large tomatoes chopped
10	cherry tomatoes
10	baby brinjals
4	drumsticks cut into 4 pieces each
2	capsicums, sliced
1/2	cup vinegar
1/2	cup jaggery
1/2	cup fresh coriander washed chopped

12	large Kashmiri chillies	
1/2	coconut freshly grated	
2	tablespoons cumin seeds	grind
1	large pod garlic	together
8	black peppercorns	in 1/2 cup
1	tablespoon Parsi dhansakh masala	vinegar
1	tsp. mustard seeds	
1	tablespoon raw mango pickle sambar powder	

1	sprig curry leaves
4	slit green chillies
1	cup sesame oil
1	cup refined oil
	salt

1. Wash pomfret and prawns separately, apply salt and set aside.

2. Grind coconut, garlic, Kashmiri chillies, cumin seeds, mustard seeds, pepper corns and masalas with the vinegar on a grinding stone or in a mixer.

3. Put the sesame oil, onions and curry leaves in a heavy flat bottomed vessel and allow the leaves to crackle. Cook till onions are soft. Add chopped tomatoes, the ground masala, slit green chillies to the pan and cook over gentle heat.

When a tantalizing aroma arises out of the masala add the prawns and cook them over a slow fire. Add 2 cups of water. When the prawns are cooked add the fish and crushed jaggery. Roll the dish from side to side by holding the vessel with 2 cloth pieces. Do not stir with a spoon. Add more salt only if necessary as the pomfret and prawns are already salted. Add cherry tomatoes. Remove from the fire.

4. Cut the brinjals into four pieces. Retain from the stalk. Place in salted water. Cut the capsicums into slices. Heat one cup refined oil in a frying pan or kadhai. Fry the baby brinjals and allow the oil to drain on a plate. Put the capsicum slices in the same pan and remove immediately from the oil. Boil the drumsticks in salted water and set aside. Chop the coriander.

5. Serve the patia fish by placing the prawns, fish slices and gravy on a flat dish. Decorate it with the fried baby brinjals, capsicums, drumsticks and coriander. Serve with hot parathas or yellow Parsi dal and white rice.

BHARUCHI AKOORI

(Savoury scrambled eggs with nuts)

Preparation Time: 10 mins.
Cooking Time: 15 mins. • Serves: 8

16	eggs
1	cup milk or cream
5	onions sliced finely
3	tablespoons coriander, chopped
2	teaspoons green chillies, chopped finely
2	large tomatoes skinned, deseeded and finely chopped
1	teaspoon ginger–garlic paste
$1/4$	teaspoon black pepper powder
$1/2$	cup raisins, fried
$1/2$	cup almonds, sliced and fried
$1/2$	cup pistachios, sliced and fried
	salt to taste
	ghee or oil for frying

1. Place oil in a kadhai. Deep fry the sliced onions till golden brown. Place tomatoes, green chillies, ginger-garlic paste and black pepper in a heavy bottomed pan. Add 4 tablespoons of oil from the kadhai in which the onions were fried. Cook on a slow fire till the tomatoes are soft. Add salt to taste and half the coriander.

2. Beat the eggs well and add the milk or cream as required. Add the beaten egg mixture with the fried onions to the cooked tomato mixture along with half the raisins, almonds and pistachios. Stir the pan vigorously with a slotted spoon till the mixture becomes firm and pulpy like yoghurt. It should not be allowed to dry up. It should remain loose yet not be watery.

3. Quickly transfer onto a serving dish and decorate with the remaining raisins, nuts and coriander. Serve with buttered toast and jam as a breakfast item or with rotis or parathas for lunch or dinner.

SADO RAVO

(Simple Semolina)

Preparation Time: 5 mins.
Cooking Time: 30 mins. • Serves 6-10

2	litres milk
100	gms. rava or semolina
2	cups sugar
4	green skinned cardamoms coarsely pounded
1	teaspoon nutmeg-cardamom coarsely pounded
$1/4$	cup fried almond flakes
$1/2$	cup fried seedless red raisins
1	teaspoon vanilla essence
$1/2$	cup pure ghee

1. Take a very heavy bottomed pan. Put in half cup pure ghee and the semolina. Mix thoroughly and then place over a slow fire. Stir the mixture round and round till a warm ivory colour tints the semolina.

2. Add 2 cups water and 2 cups sugar and stir to a smooth thick paste. Add the milk and keep stirring. Raise the heat on the stove till the milk mixture starts boiling.

3. Lower flame and keep stirring non-stop till the milk mixture becomes thick and satiny like porridge. Taste it for sufficient sugar and check that it is cooked and remove from the fire.

4. Beat in the nutmeg and cardamom powder and vanilla essence and pour into a glass bowl. Top with almonds and raisins.

I often add the petals of a pink rose.

RAVO
(Sweet Semolina)

Preparation Time: 7 mins.
Cooking Time: 40-55 mins.   •   Serves 50

This is a dish made in every Parsi home on weddings, birthdays and navjotes and it is very popular with old and young alike.

7	litres fresh, creamy milk
1	kg. rava or semolina
1	kg. 700 gms. sugar
1	kg. 500 gms. ghee
3	tablespoons cardamom and nutmeg powder
2	teaspoons vanilla essence
25	gms. pistachios
100	gms. almonds
150	gms. charoli
300	gms. seedless raisins
1½	litres water
1	pink rose
4	tablespoons ghee

1. Boil the pistachios and almonds separately. Skin and cut finely into slices.

2. Take a large flat bottomed dekchi. Place the ghee and rava in it, and allow to cook on a slow fire until the rava has absorbed all the ghee. Keep frying till a nice ivory colour is obtained. Then add the water and sugar and keep stirring till all the sugar has melted and a thick mixture forms. Keep stirring all the while and pour the milk in a steady trickle till all of it has been used up. Raise the flame and keep stirring for another 15-20 minutes till a thick liquid forms. Taste it and check that it is cooked. Sprinkle the nutmeg and cardamom powder into the milk mixture. Do not allow the rava to burn or form granules. When thick and sticky remove from the fire and mix in the vanilla essence and immediately pour into glass dishes or silver salvers.

3. Place 4 tablespoons ghee in a frying pan and fry the charoli, pistas and almonds lightly. Toss the raisins in the hot ghee and immediately lower the flame. Remove as soon as they begin to puff up. Sprinkle lavishly on the rava along with all the other nuts and some pink rose petals.

SWEET HOT TEA WITH LEMON GRASS, FRESH PEPPERMINT AND MINT

Cooking Time: 10 mins.   •   Serves: 10

For ten cups of tea you will need

8	cups of water
4	long leaves of lemon grass especially the thick portion above the root
4-8	leaves of fresh peppermint
4-8	leaves of fresh mint
4	heaped teaspoons of high quality tea

If you are using long leafed tea add two more teaspoons of tea.

Take a kettle and fill it with eight cups of water. Allow the water to boil. Wash the herbs and then pinch them, crush them and add to the boiling water. After two minutes add the four teaspoons of tea to the boiling aromatic water. Allow to boil for two minutes and pour it into a china teapot. Serve with sugar and milk.

MALIDO

Malido is a traditional Parsi sweet dish. Its importance lies in the fact that since centuries, generation after generation of priests have included it amongst the flowers and fruits placed in polished silver, circular trays and prayed over them amidst heaps of sandalwood chips and incense. All death anniversaries which the priests dedicately prayed for were accompanied by these trays of "darun", flat leaven cakes, "papri" stiff fried puries, "malido" this gorgeous concoction of sugar, flour, semolina, spices, nuts, sweets, raisins, crystal sugar and eggs. Then came the indispensable "daram" or pomegranate, without which no religious tray of fruits was complete. Then oranges, sweet limes, papaya, pineapple, apples, raisins, dates and shelled tender coconut halves were used.

After the prayers were over, those who had assembled all took "chasni". They all tasted the prayed-over sweets and fruit. Everyone had a piece of the "darun" with "malido" and tasted the pomegranate.

Even today no "baj" or prayer ceremony for the dead is complete without malido. My friend Shirinbai's preparation is the best that there is!! I share the recipe with you.

SHIRINBAI PANTHAKY NO EDA NO MALIDO

(Shrinbai Panthaky's Malido)

Preparation Time: 25 mins.
Cooking Time: 1 hr. • Serves 10-12

2 cups rava or semolina
1 cup wheat flour
3 cups sugar
6 eggs – optional
25 gms. almonds, boiled, sliced and fried
25 gms. charoli, fried
25 gms. raisins, fried
50 gms. orange peel
25 gms. sugar crystals
25 gms. jujubes
1 tablespoon cardamom – nutmeg powder
2 tablespoons extra pure ghee for frying the rotlis
500 gms. pure ghee
1 teaspoon vanilla essence

1. Mix the rava and wheat flour with two tablespoons ghee and one cup water. Mix and knead into a firm dough. Make five rotlis out of this dough and fry them. When they become cold pound the rotlis into powder.

2. Place three cups of sugar in a pan along with two cups of water. Boil and make a thick syrup, lower the flame and add the pounded rotli powder into the syrup. Keep stirring non-stop, adding all the remaining ghee little by little. Remove from the stove and cool a little.

3. If using eggs, whisk and pour into the mixture in a thin stream mixing all the while. Replace on the stove over a low fire and keep stirring vigorously for 15 to 20 minutes. Remove from the stove. Add the cardamom and nutmeg powder and vanilla essence. Stir and remove into a fancy glass dish. Mix in

half the fried nuts, orange peel and raisins.

4. Sprinkle the top of the malido liberally with the remaining half of the fried nuts, raisins, orange peel, jujubes and sugar crystals.

KHAMAN-NA-LADWA

(Cornflour Coconut Laddoos)

Preparation Time: 15 mins.
Cooking Time: 1 hr.　•　Makes 20-25

This is not an easy item to make but it is a delicious sweet. Coconut is cooked in sugar and is packed in a soft, white covering made out of rose water and cooked cornflour.

For the Stuffing
1　grated fresh coconut
8　tablespoons sugar or as per taste
1　tablespoon almonds boiled, skinned and chopped
1　tablespoon pistas boiled, skinned and chopped
2　tablespoons raisins, washed
$1/2$　teaspoon cardamom – nutmeg powder
4　tablespoons water
1　tablespoon ghee
$1/2$　teaspoon vanilla essence

1. Place the grated coconut, sugar, ghee and water into a pan and allow to cook over a slow fire till the coconut mixture loses all its water – but is still moist. Add the raisins, nuts and spice powder and stir well and remove from the fire. Set aside after mixing in the vanilla.

For the Cornflour covering
Coconut milk from 1 freshly grated coconut
150 gms. cornflour
1　litre milk
4　tablespoons sugar
1　tablespoon ghee
1　cup rose water

1. Place the cornflour in a dekchi. Add the milk and coconut milk and stir well. Then add the ghee, sugar and rose water and place on the fire and keep stirring non-stop till the mixture thickens and solidifies. Take it out in a thali and knead it to remove any granules.

2. Make about 20-25 small balls from the mixture. Place one ball in your oiled palm and pat it into a circular shape and stuff it with one tablespoon of the coconut mixture and make a round ball of it. Place it in a greased metal colander. After all the ladwas are placed in the colander, fit it over a half filled dekchi of hot water. Allow the water to boil and cover the ladwas with a damp, white muslin cloth. Then cover the colander with a lid. Do not allow the steam to escape. Cook over steam for at least half an hour.

3. Cool and chill the ladwas before eating.

RICE KHEER

Rice Kheer like Ravo was also placed amongst the food offered to the dead which was prayed over by the priests. "Malido", "darun" and "papri" were de rigueur but these sweet items like Kheer were extras included amongst the fruits.

On special "muktad" days, the last ten days of the year, special tables were set up in the Fire Temple, with soft cloth, kustis and silver vessels bearing flowers such as roses, jasmine, tuberoses or "gulcheris", gladioli and asters. The dead were and are remembered each day with prayers and ceremonies and the last day of the year was "Pateti" the day of rememberance and sorrow. It was the day on which all Parsis repented their bad thoughts, words and deeds and prayed for a good and prosperous New Year. The New Year day was "Navroze", which was celebrated by wearing new clothes and jewellery, tucking into a large breakfast of sev, dahi and sweets and going to the Fire Temples to offer thanks. The rest of the day was spent feasting and visiting friends. Nowadays, modern Parsis go to dances and movies.

CHOKHA NI KHEER

(Rice Kheer)

Preparation Time: 5 mins.
Cooking Time: 35-45 min. • Serves 6

200 gms. broken basmati rice
2 litres of milk
3 cups sugar
$\frac{1}{2}$ teaspoon rose essence
$\frac{1}{2}$ teaspoon cardamom-nutmeg powder
7-10 rose petals, preferably pink
$\frac{1}{2}$ cup raisins
silver sheets or vark (optional)

1. Soak the rice in a dekchi of cold water. Wash thoroughly. Place in a pressure cooker with 4 cups of water and cook till soft. Mash the rice.

2. Pour the milk in a large, thick, flat bottomed pan and bring to a boil. Add sufficient sugar so that the milk becomes sweet. Add the mashed up rice to the milk and allow to simmer, stirring all the time for atleast 20 to 30 minutes. Wash the raisins and add to the hot kheer.

3. Taste for sugar. Allow the kheer to cool and then add the rose essence and the spice powder. Pour into a glass dish and top with the rose petals. Serve it as cold as possible.

4. If you have cream, top the dish with beaten cream or silver sheets if so desired.

KHEER-KESAR-NI

(Saffron Kheer)

Preparation Time: 5 mins.
Cooking Time: 45-50 mins. • Serves 6

2   gms. saffron
2   litres of rich creamy milk
3   cups sugar
1   cup broken basmati rice
1   teaspoon nutmeg-cardamom powder
100 gms. charoli or 100 gms. almonds boiled
200 gms. raisins
     silver leaf

1. Wash rice and cook till soft in 3 cups of water in a pressure cooker. Mix vigorously till the rice grains are mashed.

2. Heat the milk in a flat, wide mouthed vessel. Add the sugar, bring to the boil and then add the rice mixture and allow to cook over a slow heat. Wash and add the raisins to the rice.

3. Meanwhile, heat the kesar and soak it in a cup of hot milk. Stir with a teaspoon and add to the rice mixture on the stove. Do not allow the mixture to stand but keep stirring till the milk is reduced to half its quantity. Add the spice powder.

4. Cool and chill. Serve in little silver bowls topped with charoli or almonds. Taste for sugar before removing from the fire. If necessary cover with silver leaf.

GHEHU-NU-DUDH

(Wheat-Milk Sweet)

Preparation Time: 30 mins.
Cooking Time: 30-40 Mins. • Serves 6

250 gms. dried wheat milk
250 gms. sugar
2   litres milk
50   gms. almonds boiled and sliced
50   gms. raisins washed, dried
1/2 cup rose water
1/2 teaspoon nutmeg-cardamom powder
100 gms. pure ghee

1. Wet the dried wheat milk in two cups of water for half an hour.

2. Place the pure ghee in a vessel and when hot pour in the dissolved dried milk and water and briskly stir the mixture for five minutes. Add sugar and milk and keep stirring till the mixture thickens and looks like scrambled eggs. When all the milk has been absorbed taste for sugar and if fully cooked remove from the fire.

3. Mix in the raisins, almonds, rose water and nutmeg-cardamom powder and briskly mix for one minute before emptying the mixture into a glass dish.

Dhan Dar   (13
Chamna Ne Kolmi No Patio   (14

FALOODA

This wonderful drink must have been brought by Parsis from their homeland in Iran. Its wonderful composition consists of rose sherbet or syrup, sweet milk, little black tukmaria seeds, cooked wheat milk drops, cream or ice-cream. Its another item which is enjoyed on the 21st of March each year. This day is the Spring Equinox and was widely celebrated in Iran. Even today, in India, the Irani Zoroastrians and Parsis celebrate this day as Jamshedi Navroze in memory of an old Iranian King who was a law maker and who is said to have discovered the Equinoxes as well as the power of wine.

My mother makes Falooda faithfully every 21st March and I must admit it beats the Falooda made in the best of all restaurants.

Preparation Time: 10 mins.
Cooking Time: 40 mins. • Serves 16

1   bottle rose syrup
1   block vanilla or strawberry ice-cream
$1/2$ cup rose water
12   glasses milk
2   cups sugar
$1/4$ cup tukmaria seeds
300 gms. dried wheat-milk powder

1. Soak the tukmaria seeds in four cups of water in a small vessel the day before and place in the refrigerator.

2. Soak the wheat milk in a large vessel in two cups of water, half cup sugar, half cup rose water and when dissolved place over a medium flame. Stir non-stop till you get a thick glutinous gel. This will take 30 minutes to cook.

3. Keep prepared before hand a dekchi over which you can place a colander. Break two kilos of ice and place in the dekchi along with 2 cups of water. As soon as the wheat milk is cooked as thick as possible, place it in the colander and stir it with a ladle so that beads of wheat milk fall into the icy water and firm up immediately. If you do not use ice the beads will disintegrate and become a soggy mass. When all the mixture has been used up, place the vessel containing the beads in the refrigerator.

4. Take the milk, add sugar to it, mix and heat in a large vessel. Keep stirring till the milk thickens and remove after 20 minutes or so. Cool and refrigerate.

5. To assemble the Falooda, take 16 fancy, tall glasses. Place one tablespoon of swollen tukmaria seeds in each glass. Then place one tablespoon of wheat milk beads over the seeds. Then fill 1" of rose syrup in every glass. Pour milk in the glass till it is three-quarter full. Top with a scoop of ice-cream and serve.

Rayo   (16)
Lagan-Nu-Custard   (4)
Mitthoo Dahi   (13)
Dodhi-No-Murambo   (7)
Parsi Sev   (12)

TAL-NA-LADWA

(Sesame Laddoos)

Preparation Time: Overnight
Cooking Time: 25-30 mins. • Serves 10-15

500 gms. white sesame seeds
500 gms. best quality jaggery
100 gms. small kaju pieces roasted
50 gms. kopra finely sliced and chopped
1   teaspoon ground cardamom powder
      ghee

1. The sesame seeds must be soaked in water overnight. The next morning they must be drained and all the water wiped out by squeezing them in a piece of white muslin cloth. Spread them out to dry in the sun and when quite dry squeeze them between both palms.

2. Roast the sesame seeds on a tava on a low fire. They must not discolour. Roast the kaju pieces on the same tava.

3. Heat the jaggery and allow it to melt. When it begins to boil, remove it from the fire and mix in the sesame seeds, kaju pieces, kopra pieces and the ground cardamom powder. Pour the mixture in a tray or thali.

4. Grease both palms with ghee or oil. Make tiny balls, smaller than sour limes, whilst the mixture is still warm. Be careful not to burn your fingers. Press the balls well so they do not break.

SOOTHANOO

(Dried Ginger Sweet)

Preparation Time: 3 mins.
Cooking Time: 30 mins. • Serves 10

400 gms. sugar
100 gms. dried, powdered dill or suva seeds
25 gms. dried, powdered ginger
10 gms. khaskhas or poppy seeds
1   teaspoon rice flour
1   teaspoon cardamom seeds – crushed
      pure ghee

1. Grease an aluminium tray with one tablespoon ghee and set aside.

2. Make a thick syrup with 4 cups of water and the sugar. Squeeze a tablespoon of sour lime juice in the hot syrup. With a perforated spoon remove the scum which will surface over the syrup and drain it through a damp muslin cloth into another clean vessel. Add all the ingredients into the thick syrup and stir the mixture non-stop over a low flame. When it thickens pour it into the greased tray and level it with a spatula. Cut lines into the sweet and when cool break it into pieces.

SAALAM PAAK

(Milk Sweet)

Preparation Time: 15 mins.
Cooking Time: 45 mins.–1 hr. • Serves 10

2   litres creamy milk – boiled once
1   kg. sugar
1   kg. pure ghee
400 gms. almonds, boiled, skinned, sliced
100 gms. each 4 types of magaj seeds, of dudhi,
     pumpkin, cucumber and melon
100 gms. punjabi saalam
1   teaspoon nutmeg powder
1   tablespoon cardamom powder
1   bottle rose water

1. Make a thick syrup with the sugar, rose water and 3 cups water.

2. Fry half the almonds till light brown in a little ghee and set aside.

3. Place the ghee in a vessel and fry all the different magaj and the remaining almonds and when light red, remove from the fire and pound them finely. The saalam should also be ground very fine.

4. Now comes the difficult part. Take some ghee about one cup from the vessel in which the almonds had been fried and place it in a clean vessel. Heat it and put in the saalam powder, lower flame and mix vigorously. Do not stop. Get someone to pour the milk in a thin stream and keep mixing vigorously, otherwise nodules will form in the milk.

5. Keep stirring non-stop after all the milk has been used up. Pour all the leftover ghee in which the almonds were fried into the pan and the sugar syrup until it becomes like mava. Mix in the almond slices and the 4 magaj which have been fried and pounded, nutmeg and cardamom powders. Pour into a greased dish and serve when cooled.

GAJJAR-NO-HALWO

(Carrot Halwa)

Preparation Time: 25 mins.
Cooking Time: 30-40 mins. • Serves 10

500 gms. red carrots, grated
500 gms. sugar
100 gms mava
2   cups milk
1   teaspoon nutmeg-cardamom powder
3   tablespoons raisins
2   tablespoons almonds, boiled, skinned, sliced
     silver leaf
$\frac{1}{2}$ cup pure ghee

1. Add sugar and carrots to 2 cups milk and cook over medium heat till carrots are soft. Add mawa, cardamom and nutmeg powder and the ghee and stir non-stop till the halwa slowly starts separating from the ghee. Add the washed raisins and sliced almonds, stir for a further five minutes.

2. Place in a fancy dish and cover with silver leaf. Serve warm or chilled.

GAJJAR-NO-MURAMBO

(Carrot Marmalade)

Preparation Time: 35-40 mins.
Cooking Time: 45 mins.–1 hr. • Serves 20

2   kgs. large red carrots, grated
3   kgs. sugar
2   tablespoons lime juice
1   teaspoon cardamom seeds
300 gms. seedless raisins

1. Take large red carrots. Trim off the tops and tips and cut into two halves lengthwise. Remove the central greenish-yellow pith and discard. Grate and weigh upto two kilos.

2. Place the sugar in a large clean pan and add two litres of water. Heat and when the syrup boils add two tablespoons of lime juice. Remove the scum from the surface with a perforated spoon and strain through a muslin cloth into a clean vessel. Place the syrup on the fire and when it boils add the grated carrots and lower the flame. Keep stirring till the carrots become soft and the syrup is totally absorbed. Add the cardamom seeds.

3. Wash the raisins and add them to the carrots in the vessel. Taste for sugar and tenderness. Remove from the fire, cool and serve in a fancy dish.

DODHI–NO–HALWO

(Large White Ash Gourd Halwa)

Preparation Time: 45 mins.
Cooking Time: 1 hr. • Serves: 20

2   kgs. white pumpkin, grated
1$\frac{1}{2}$ kg. sugar
1$\frac{1}{2}$ litre milk
$\frac{1}{2}$ litre thick cream
25   gms. almonds, sliced
25   gms. pistachios, sliced
7   drops green food colouring
10   green cardamoms, seeds only

1. Skin the pumpkin and grate the flesh discarding all woolly pulp and seeds. Squeeze the grated flesh between both your palms and allow the juice to trickle out.

2. Place the pumpkin in a heavy based pan along with the juice and cook till soft. Add milk and stir with a wooden spoon over a medium flame. Keep stirring non-stop till the pumpkin begins to soften and the milk evaporates. Add cream, sugar and the cardamom seeds and stir over a low flame till the mixture thickens and is the consistency of marmalade. When soft and sweet to the taste, remove the pan from the fire and add the green colouring and mix well.

3. Pour into a dish, decorate with fried almond and pistachio slices and refrigerate.

KACCHI-KERI-NO-MURAMBO

(Raw Mango Marmalade)

Preparation Time: 4 hrs.
Cooking Time: 40 mins. – 1 hr. • Serves: 20

2   kgs. grated raw rajapuri large mangoes
3   kgs. sugar
1   teaspoon cardamom seeds
1   raw egg (optional)

1. Place grated mangoes in a clean stainless steel vessel and cover with cold water for 3 hours. Drain in a colander and allow to dry for half an hour.

2. Place the sugar in a large vessel and crush the egg with its shell thoroughly till it is totally one with the sugar. Add two litres of water and place the vessel on a medium flame. When the mixture boils, lift the vessel from the fire and remove the scum on the surface of the liquid. Then wet a muslin cloth and strain the liquid into a clean vessel.

3. Put the sugar syrup on medium heat and add the grated mangoes and keep stirring till the muramba thickens. Add the cardamom seeds and when the syrup has dried up remove from the fire. Store in a glass airtight jar when cool.

BAFELA SAFARCHAN

(Stewed Apples)

Preparation Time: 7 mins.
Cooking Time: 25-30 mins. • Serves: 6-8

9   large apples
2   cups sugar
3   cups water
3   green cardamom seeds
1   sour lime

1. Peel, core and chop the fruit and sprinkle with the sour lime juice.

2. Place apples, sugar and water in a sauce pan and bring to a boil. Add the cardamom seeds. Simmer for 15 minutes. Remove from the fire, cool and chill.

3. Serve with blancmange or cream.

DUDH-NI-SEV

(Vermicelli cooked in Milk)

Preparation Time: 5 mins.
Cooking Time: 25-30 mins. • Serves: 6

250 gms. vermicelli
250 gms. sugar
1   teaspoon rose essence
$1/2$ teaspoon cardamom seeds
$1^1/_2$ litre milk

1. Place the vermicelli in a vessel after breaking it into 2" pieces along with three teacups of water. When the vermicelli boils and swells and is soft to the touch drain the water and add the milk, sugar and cardamom seeds and allow to thicken over a slow fire for 10 minutes.

2. Remove from the fire, add the rose essence and cool. Serve with rose petals.

BADAM NA MAKRUM

(Almond Macaroons)

Preparation Time: 20 mins.
Cooking Time: 35-40 mins. • Makes: 30-40

1	kg. very fine castor sugar
$\frac{1}{2}$	kg. almonds, boiled skinned
8	egg whites
$\frac{1}{2}$	teacup rose water
$\frac{1}{2}$	teaspoon cardamom seeds
	butter

1. Grind the boiled almonds along with the rose water in a mixer until you have a coarsely ground mixture.

2. Heat oven to 350°F. Take a tray and spread brown paper on it. Butter it.

3. Whip the egg whites with a pinch of salt till you get stiff peaks. Then place the sugar and almonds in a bowl and mix thoroughly. Gradually add the egg whites and cardamom seeds till all the egg white has blended with the sugar and almond mixture.

4. Place teaspoonfuls of mixture at a distance of two or one and a half inches away from each other and bake till brown. This will take 15-20 minutes in a pre-heated oven, depending on the size of your macaroons.

NARIEL NA MAKRUM

(Coconut Macaroons)

Preparation Time: 15 mins.
Cooking Time: 25 mins. • Makes: 30-40

500	gms. coconut, finely grated
250	gms. castor sugar
6	egg whites
1	teaspoon vanilla essence
	butter

1. Grease a baking tin with butter and set aside. Heat the oven to 350°F.

2. Mix the castor sugar and grated coconut and vanilla essence in a large bowl.

3. Beat the egg whites with a pinch of salt till stiff peaks rise and gently fold into the coconut-sugar mixture.

4. Place teaspoons of mixture on the buttered tray leaving space between each teaspoonful and bake till golden brown.

BADAM PAAK

(Almond Halwa)

Preparation Time: 15 mins.
Cooking Time: 45-50 mins. • Serves 7-10

350 gms. castor sugar
250 gms. almonds
125 gms. pure ghee
50 gms. pistachios
$\frac{1}{2}$ litre thick cream
$\frac{1}{2}$ litre milk
1 cup rose water
1 gm. saffron

1. Boil almonds for ten minutes. Cool, skin and fry in a little ghee till pale pink in colour. Grind with a little rose water and set aside.

2. Beat cream and milk with a whisk and place in a heavy bottomed vessel over a low flame. Stir non-stop till reduced to half taking care not to allow the bottom to burn. Remove from fire when milk starts to thicken.

3. Dissolve the sugar in half a cup each of plain water and rose water and bring to a boil. Cool and boil again. Add saffron, the sugar water and ground almonds to the cream and mix vigorously.

4. Grease a tray with butter and keep ready.

5. Increase the heat to medium and mix in circular movements till it thickens. Immediately empty into the geased tray and pat the surface to a level thickness.

6. Mark into small squares whilst still warm.

KOPRA PAAK

(Coconut Sweet)

Preparation Time: 5 mins.
Cooking Time: 20-25 mins. • Serves 7-10

2 freshly grated coconuts
  Sugar the weight of the grated coconuts
50 gms. sliced almonds
8 green cardamoms, seeds removed
1 cup rose water
10 drops red colour-cochineal
2 tablespoons ghee

1. Place the grated coconut, sugar, rose water and the cardamom seeds in a heavy pan over a medium flame and stir continuously with a wooden spoon. Allow the mixture to thicken till it reaches the soft ball stage.

2. Add the cochineal drops, mix well and pour into a flat greased glass dish. Cool and cut into squares. Top with sliced almonds.

MITTHA TOAST

(French Toast)

Preparation Time: 15 mins.
Cooking Time: 25 mins. • Makes: 12 Toasts.

12	large slices bakery bread
$1\frac{1}{4}$	litre creamy milk
2	cups sugar
4	eggs
1	tablespoon nutmeg-cardamom powder
1	tablespoon vanilla essence
	pure ghee or refined oil or vanaspati ghee

1. Heat the milk, add half a cup of sugar, bring to the boil and pour into a large tray with high sides.

2. Whisk the eggs along with the spice powder and vanilla and mix into the milk. Soak the bread slices in the milk and overturn once.

3. Put oil or ghee into a large frying pan. When the ghee is hot, place as many slices as you can conveniently manage into the frying pan. When the lower side of the slice is golden coloured, turn and fry the top side. Sprinkle the cooked side with sugar and pick up the slice with a spatula and place in a dish with the sugar side down. Sugar the top of the slice and continue frying in batches till all the bread slices have been fried and sugared. The toasts should be moist and not dry. Do not fry like purees.

This recipe can be cooked for breakfast, brunch or tea. My great grandfather was very fond of these toasts and as a child I remember going to a tiny village in Gujarat, with hampers of food amongst which were two biscuit tins full of toasts. I can never forget the pleasure the old gentleman used to derive from these toasts because 50 years ago no bread was available in his area.

BHAKRAS

(Sweet Fried Cookies)

Preparation Time: 1 hr.
Cooking Time: 20-25 mins. • Makes 42

2	teacups sugar
2	teacups maida or self raising flour
1	teacup wheat flour
50	gms. curds
2	eggs
2	tablespoons ghee
1	teaspoon vanilla
$\frac{1}{2}$	teaspoon baking powder
1	teaspoon nutmeg–cardamom powder
	ghee for frying at least half kg.

1. Take a large thali. Crack the eggs in it and mix in the curds and sugar and beat it all together with your hand till the sugar melts. Add vanilla and spice powder.

2. Gradually add one tablespoon ghee and the baking powder, self-raising and wheat flour and mix well till you get a resilient dough.

3. Cover with a damp cloth for half an hour.

4. Roll out large thick rounds like flat chappatis $\frac{1}{4}$" thick on a large wooden board. Take a water glass, or biscuit cutter and cut rounds into the thick chappatis.

5. Place ghee in a kadhai or fry pan and when the ghee gets hot, lower the flame and pop one round into it. If the bhakra floats on top and does not sink, the ghee is ready for deep frying. Fry 3–5 at a time and when red–brown remove from the ghee. You will be able to make about 42 bhakras from the above amount.

6. Serve as tea time snacks.

BADAM-NE-PISTA-NI-CHIKKI

(Almond and Pista Toffee)

Preparation Time: 5 mins.
Cooking Time: 20-25 mins.

500 gms. sugar
75 gms. whole almonds
75 gms. shelled pistachios
1   cup rose water
3   green cardamoms, seeds removed
1   tablespoon butter
1   sour lime

1. Place sugar and rose water in a pan and allow sugar to melt. Squeeze juice from the sour lime and remove all the scum which will collect on top of the syrup. Add the cardamom seeds.
2. Boil the syrup till a drop hardens when dropped in water. Add the nuts and mix well. Quickly pour the mixture onto a small greased tray. Cut into small squares whilst still warm.

MUMRA-NI-CHIKKI

(Puffed Rice Toffee)

Preparation Time: 3 mins.
Cooking Time: 15 mins.

500 gms. puffed rice
125 gms. jaggery
$^1/_2$ teaspoon dried ginger powder
    pinch of salt
1   tablespoon ghee

1. Grate or mash the jaggery and place in a heavy pan along with the ghee on low medium heat till it dissolves. Allow to boil, quickly remove the pan from the stove and mix in the puffed rice, salt and ginger powder.

2. Empty the toffee onto a greased tray and dab it down with a greased palm till the surface is level. Make squares with a knife before the toffee hardens.

KARKARIA

(Banana Fritters)

Preparation Time: 15 mins.
Cooking Time: 15 mins. • Serves 4-6

3   green skinned ripe bananas weighing 200 gms.
200 gms. sugar
200 gms. maida
100 gms. wheat flour
25 gms. raisins
2   eggs
$^1/_2$ teaspoon vanilla essence
$^1/_2$ teaspoon cardamom-nutmeg powder
    ghee

1. Mash the bananas. Add the sugar, essence and cardamom-nutmeg powder. Beat in the eggs and whisk the mixture well.
2. Gradually add in wheat flour, maida and the raisins.
3. Heat half a kadhai of ghee and when it gets hot, lower the flame and take one tablespoonful of mixture at a time and gently lower it into the ghee. It will puff up and when it becomes golden brown in colour turn over with the help of two forks and allow to cook through. Do not over fry. Drain on an absorbent paper and serve immediately with tea.

MAWA NA PAANCAKE
(Mawa Pancakes)

Preparation Time: 45 mins.
Cooking Time: 25 mins. • Serves: 6

For Pancake Mix:
250 gms. maida
1 dessertspoon castor sugar
1 dessertspoon ghee
$\frac{1}{2}$ teaspoon vanilla
2 eggs
2 cups milk

For Mawa Filling:
250 gms. mawa
4 tablespoons milk
1 teaspoon vanilla
$\frac{1}{4}$ teaspoon nutmeg-cardamom powder
150 gms. powdered sugar or to taste
10 gms. almonds

1. In a large bowl mix together eggs, sugar and ghee to a smooth paste.

2. Add vanilla and then add the flour in a steady trickle adding the milk as required. When the milk and flour are both used up and a smooth paste is obtained, cover the bowl and set aside for 30-35 minutes.

3. Blanche almonds and grind coarsely or chop finely and add to the mawa which should be warmed and stirred smooth with a little milk in a clean glass bowl. Now add the vanilla and the nutmeg-cardamom powder and stir well alongwith the powdered sugar. Reheat gently for five minutes.

4. Take a medium sized frying pan and grease the surface all over with $\frac{1}{4}$ teaspoon ghee. When hot put one dessertspoon or serving spoonful of the pancake mixture and tilt from side to side. When the bottom side is cooked flip the pancake over and cook the other side. When both sides are done put on to a plate. Spoon some mawa mixture on to its centre and fold up the four sides like an envelope.

5. Khaman-na-ladwa mixture can be substituted if desired instead of the mawa as the latter is not always available. Even khajoor-ghari mix may be used as a filling.

MATHURA NA PENDA
(Penda)

Preparation Time: 10 mins.
Cooking Time: 25-30 mins. • Serves: 10

500 gms. mawa
500 gms. powdered sugar
2 gms. saffron
3 tablespoons warm milk
200 gms. pure ghee

1. Heat the saffron on a tawa and crumble it in the warm milk.

2. Break up the mawa in a tray and crumble it or grate it. Place it in a clean vessel and shake it up and down over a medium flame. Once the mawa lightens up add the powdered sugar and the saffron milk. Mix continuously until both items have assimilated well. When the mawa becomes ivory coloured add the ghee and immediately spread the mixture on a tray and make into tiny balls whilst still very warm. Flatten the mawa ball on top by pressing a finger on the top surface. Cool and serve.

POPATJEE

(An unusual Parsi sweet dunked in sugar syrup)

You can only make this sweet if you have a special fry pan Popatjee No Penno with five or six holes in it. My mother used toddy to make these sweet balls. If toddy is not available you can use fresh yeast from the baker or curds.

Preparation Time: 4½ hrs.
Cooking Time: 40 mins.–1 hr. • Makes 30

1 kg. sugar, syrup made with 2 gms. saffron or 5 tablespoons rose water
500 gms. wheat flour
25 gms. fresh bakers yeast
50 gms. finely chopped orange peel
1 teaspoon cardamom seeds, coarsely ground
1 teaspoon carraway seeds, coarsely ground
2 tablespoons seedless raisins, washed, dried
2 tablespoons almonds, boiled, skinned, chopped and coarsely ground
½ litre milk
5 eggs
   pure ghee or vanaspati

1. Break the eggs into a deep glass bowl and whisk them. Add two tablespoons ghee and the yeast and mix well. Add the milk and mix again.

2. Place the flour in a liquidiser and pour the mixture into it and whisk well. Pour the mixture into a glass bowl, cover and keep in a warm place to rise for four hours.

3. Heat ghee in the special popatjee pan till all the holes are covered with it. Mix the raisins, nuts and spice powders into the mixture and with a small cup pour the mixture into the holes. Allow the bottom side to get golden brown and turn over. When both sides are cooked remove from the ghee and place the balls into the sugar syrup. Allow to soak well and then remove onto a flat dish. Make several batches.

CHOKHA NA ATA NOO AAOUD

(Rice Flour Sweet)

Preparation Time: 15 mins.
Cooking Time: 40-50 mins.

250 gms. rice flour
500 gms. powdered sugar
300 gms. pure ghee
25 gms. almonds boiled, skinned and sliced
50 gms. almonds boiled, skinned and finely chopped
2 large coconuts, grated
2 litres full cream milk
1 teaspoon green cardamom seeds
1 teaspoon powdered nutmeg
4 teaspoons rose essence

1. Warm the milk. Mix the grated coconuts in half a litre of milk and then remove the coconut milk by liquidising the mixture or grinding it. Discard the coconut.

2. Place the remaining milk and coconut milk in a heavy vessel. Add the sugar and stir. Place over a medium flame and when it boils, lower the flame and add the rice flour whilst stirring non-stop, with the right hand. As the milk and water evaporate the mixture will start thickening and slowly form a lump.

3. Before this happens add chopped almonds, two hundred grams ghee, cardamom seeds and nutmeg powder. Stir continuously.

4. When you feel the mixture is cooked add the rest of the ghee and rose essence. Stir vigorously and empty the hardened contents onto a well greased dish or tray. Press the mixture with a greased spatula. Sprinkle sliced almonds on top of the sweet and when cool, cut into squares. Chill.

GOR PAPRI — NO. 1

(A Jaggery Sweet)

Preparation Time: 5 mins.
Cooking Time: 12-15 mins. • Serves: 8-10

Gor Papri is very easy to make and in olden days used to be placed amongst food offerings at all religious functions. It is a cheap, healthy and nutritious sweet.

800 gms. best quality jaggery
150 gms. wheat flour
120 gms. pure ghee
1 teaspoon coarsely ground cardamom
1 teaspoon grated nutmeg
1 teaspoon vanilla essence

1. Grease a small tray with butter.
2. Chop the jaggery and place in a thick bottomed pan with two cups of water. Allow to melt over a very low flame. Add the wheat flour, ghee and spices and stir vigorously. Allow to boil. Add the essence and remove from the fire and pour immediately into the greased tray.
3. Cool and cut into squares.

GOR-PAPRI — NO. 2

(Sweet Jaggery Diamonds)

Preparation Time: 5 mins.
Cooking Time: 15-20 mins.

500 gms. best quality yellow chikki type jaggery
70 gms. wheat flour or 70 gms. rice flour
100 gms. pine nuts or 100 gms. pumpkin seeds
1 tablespoon cardamom-nutmeg powder
75 gms. ghee and extra to grease the aluminium tray

1. Chop the jaggery and place in a high sided, thick bottomed vessel. Add one cup of water and allow the jaggery to melt over a slow fire. Stir non-stop. Gently mix in the flour a little at a time. There should be no lumps. Add the ghee and allow the mixture to bubble for five minutes. Add the cardamom-nutmeg powder and if you feel the mixture is beginning to thicken pour it immediately onto a greased tray. Pat the surface flat with the bottom of a well greased flat bottomed metal bowl or broad, flat knife. Sprinkle the nuts quickly on the warm surface and pat flat with your palm. When cool cut into diamond shapes.

DAR NI PORI

Preparation Time: 1 hr.-13 mins.
Cooking Time: 25-30 mins. • Makes 2

For the Rich Crust (Maan)
100 gms. rice flour
100 gms. ghee or vanaspati
    a pinch of salt

• Place the ghee in a large round thala and stir it round and round with the palm of your hand till it liquefies. Slowly allow the rice flour and salt to trickle into the ghee and keep turning the mixture with your palm till it is well melted. Divide the mixture into two equal rounds and place in a bowl of ice-cold water.

For the Wheat flour rounds
100 gms. rava or semolina
50 gms. wheat flour
1   teaspoon ghee
$\frac{1}{2}$ cup water
1   teaspoon rose essence
    a pinch of salt

• Put the semolina, wheat flour and salt in a large thala. Add half a cup of water and mix well, kneading it as you do for chappatis. Add the rose essence and a teaspoon of ghee and knead for a further 10 minutes then divide into two rounds and set aside.

For the Dar stuffing
250 gms. toovar dar or pigeon pea dal
275 gms. sugar
2   teaspoon nutmeg and cardamom powder
1   teaspoon vanilla essence
$\frac{1}{2}$ teaspoon carraway seeds grounded
10 gms. charoli
10 gms. raisins
15 gms. crystallized cherries (finely chopped)
6   tablespoons ghee (2 for mixing + 4 for frying)

1. Place the washed toovar dar in a pressure cooker with $2\frac{1}{2}$ cups of water and cook for about 15 minutes until soft. Empty into a large vessel and add the sugar, nutmeg-cardamom powder, vanilla essence and the ghee. Mix well. Add the raisins, cherries and charoli and if the dar is not thick, heat it again and cool it until it thickens.

2. Spread one of the wheat flour rounds onto a flat surface with your fingertips till it becomes circular and is the size of a quarter plate. Then take one ball of Maan which was placed in water and spread it across the wheat flour layer making it into a flat circle roughly 5-6" in diameter. Make a disc of the other Maan and wheat flour round.

3. Divide the dar into two equal portions and place each on the two flattened layers. Fold the layer over the dar and pat the stuffed pori flat with the palm of your hand till it is 6" across.

4. Place an iron tava on the fire and put one tablespoon ghee in it. Allow to heat for 2 minutes and place one pori carefully in the centre of the tava. Allow to cook for 5 minutes on each side shifting it back and forth with two pieces of soft cloth till golden brown.

5. Cut into wedges and serve hot with tea.

KERANA PATTICE ATHWA KERVAI

(Banana Pattice stuffed with dry fruits)

Preparation Time: 8 mins.
Cooking Time: 40 mins.-1 hr.   •   Makes 24

12   large, ripe black skinned cooking bananas
1   cup sugar
$\frac{1}{2}$ cup pure ghee
$\frac{1}{2}$ cup pistachios, boiled, skinned, chopped
2   tablespoons arrowroot powder
1   cup seedless raisins, cleaned, washed
$\frac{1}{2}$ teaspoon powdered nutmeg
$\frac{1}{2}$ teaspoon powdered cardamom
1   teaspoon vanilla essence
       ghee or vanaspati for frying
$\frac{1}{2}$ cup rice flour

1. Roll the bananas, skin and cut vertically into four pieces from top to bottom. Remove the black veins from the centre of the bananas. Mash them and place them in a thick bottomed pan along with half the sugar, half the ghee and cook over a low fire stirring all the while. The bananas should become light golden in colour and be soft without any lumps. Mix the arrowroot into two tablespoons of water and add to the pan and stir till the bananas become sticky and collect into a lump. Mix in the cardamom and nutmeg powders and remove from the fire and allow to cool.

2. Place the remaining ghee in a small iron kadhai and lightly fry the nuts and raisins. Add two tablespoons water and the remaining sugar and mix well over a low fire till you get a sticky sugar syrup. When the sugar syrup thickens remove from the fire. Add vanilla essence.

3. Spread the cooked banana mixture on a thali and make equal portions. Then grease both your palms and place a ball of mashed banana on the palm of your left hand and gently press it so that you get a flat round circle. Place a teaspoon of the nut mixture in the centre of the circle and fold the banana over it. Make a tight ball so that the sugar does not leak out. Press lightly on top and bottom and lightly cover with rice flour.

4. After stuffing all the balls, heat vanaspati ghee in an iron kadhai or non-stick fry pan. When the ghee is very hot, lower the flame a little and deep fry the banana pattice, turn two to three at a time till golden brown and remove from the ghee.

MANGO MILK SHAKE

Preparation Time: 5 mins.   •   No Cooking.
Serves 6-8

6-8   ripe alphonso mangoes or ready made mango pulp
1   litre milk
       sugar to taste

1. Boil the milk with sufficient sugar to make it sweet. Simmer for seven minutes, remove from fire and cool. When cold, chill in the refrigerator.

2. Five minutes before the drinks are needed liquidize a little fresh or canned mango pulp with a quarter of the milk. In this manner liquidise all the pulp alongwith the chilled milk.

3. Serve in tall glasses whilst still frothy.

KHAJOOR NI GHARI

(Date Pastry)

Preparation Time: 1 hr.
Cooking Time: 30 mins. • Makes 5 Pastry Cakes

For the Maan (Crust)
50   gms. rice flour
50   gms. ghee
1   teaspoon rose essence
      a pinch of salt

1. Spread the ghee in a thala with the help of your palm. Sprinkle the rice flour and salt thereon and knead till soft. Make 5 equal balls and place them in a bowl of ice-water.

For the Dough
150 gms. wheat flour
100 gms. ghee
1   teaspoon rose essence
     a pinch of salt

2. Put the wheat flour, salt, rose essence and ghee in the thala. Mix well and add half a teacup of water. Knead for 5 minutes and divide into 5 equal balls.

For the Date Stuffing
500 gms. mashed dates
2   tablespoons sugar
1   tablespoon ghee
2   tablespoons rose essence
7-10 coarsely ground almonds
ghee for deep frying

3. Put all the ingredients mentioned under date stuffing in a pan over a low fire and mash thoroughly for about 5 minutes.

4. Take one portion of dough and spread it on the palm of your hand. Spread one ball of Maan on top of it and fold the layers into a small flat cake. Spread this on the thala to form a circle 3" in diameter. Put one full tablespoon of the date stuffing in the centre of the flat cake and fold it over. Pat it flat into a 3" diameter cake. Repeat for the remaining portions.

5. Heat vanaspati/ghee in an iron kadhai. When hot, add the Ghari (stuffed date cake) to the ghee and deep-fry until golden brown.

6. Serve hot, with tea.

COLD MILK

Preparation Time: 15 mins.
Cooking Time: 25 mins. • Serves 6-10

2   litres milk
400 gms. sugar
3   tablespoons pistachios, boiled, ground
$\frac{1}{2}$ teaspoon vanilla essence
1   teaspoon cardamom-nutmeg powder

1. Boil the milk. Add sugar as per taste till the milk is well sweetened. Heat over a low fire for 20 minutes stirring non-stop.

2. As the milk begins to thicken add the ground pistachios. Boil for a further 10 minutes. Remove from fire, add the vanilla and cardamom-nutmeg powder. Stir and cool.

3. Divide the liquid between six to ten glasses. Cover with foil and chill well before serving.

MINOCHEHER AND TEHMI BEHRAM – KAMDIN'S METHOD FOR VARADHVARA

(Delicious Fried Wheat Cakes)

These fried dough cakes are easy to make and delicious to eat. They are to be had during the wedding season. Nowadays, practically no one makes them at home and orders are given to the local agiary or fire temple. These are made in two or three sizes, small, medium and large.

Four days before the wedding we have 'madar-sora' or engagement ceremony at the bride's house as well as the groom's house. A mango sapling is planted at the entrance. A man of the house wearing a red turban puts some curd into the flower pot which holds the mango sapling. He also adds some rice and wheat grains to the pot. Then a red handkerchief covering an envelope containing little bits of gold and silver, is tied to the tree. Fire is brought and sukhar-loban is fanned in the area to bring health and happiness to the couple.

There is a deep symbolism as regards the planting of this tree, which in ancient days used to be placed in the corner of the wedding "mandav" or mandap which was a covered area prepared for the wedding guests to dine in.

The tree ceremony was also important because it meant that no one could now stop the wedding from taking place, no matter what.

The mother-in-law did 'achoo-michu' to the tree, by breaking an egg into the pot and then a coconut was broken and its water sprinkled over the tree.

The day after this in the morning or evening the "Varadh-pattar Baj" took place in the Agiary. The satum-no-kardo prayer was recited by the priest in front of a silver thali of food. The thali contained:

3 varadhvaras
3 large sarias (rice papad)
3 large sized regular papads
3 boiled eggs
a two egg salted omelette
1 plate of gor-papdi (toffee)
1 plate of sev
1 plate of malido
3 rotlis

The dead relatives of the bride and the groom, called "asho ruvans" are remembered and they are requested to bless the young couple with health and happiness.

Then half of the food is sent by each side to the other at home.

In olden days right uptil 50 years ago, a game called akkuddi-kukkaddi was played by young girls and boys on this day.

A thala was filed with bite size pieces of all the items used in the varadh-pattar baj. Then somebody placed the thala in the courtyard and banged a thali to call the youngsters who tried to grab the food and were pelted with barrages of water.

Khaman Na Ladwa (18
Badam Na Makrum (26
Mehsoor Paak
Mummra Ni Chikki (29
Karkaria (29
Bhakras (28
Dodhi-No-Halwo (24

VARADHVARA

Preparation Time: 1 hr.
Cooking Time: 1½ hrs. • Serves 30

750 gms. best quality wheat flour
375 gms. semolina or rava
400 gms. powdered sugar
500 gms. pure ghee
1¼ teaspoons baking powder
50 gms. charoli
50 gms. almonds, boiled, skinned and chopped
1 teaspoon carraway seeds
1 teaspoon mace powder
1 teaspoon nutmeg and cardamom powder
1 tablespoon vanilla essence
5 eggs
pure ghee or vanaspati for frying

1. Place the flour, semolina, sugar, spices and melted ghee in a large thala. Mix well and then add the baking powder, whipped eggs and sufficient water to make a smooth pliable dough. The dough should not be limp or wet and should hold its shape. Taste for sweetness at this point. Add extra powdered sugar to dough if necessary.

2. Lightly fry the chopped nuts, charoli and add them along with the vanilla essence and carraway seeds to the dough. Knead the dough with the knuckles of both your hands, make a smooth ball of the dough and place it in a large vessel and cover it with a damp cloth for two hours. Place in a warm corner.

3. Divide the dough into three balls. Flatten them with your palms till you get cakes standing one inch high and round in shape and flat at the top and bottom. Do not use a rolling pin under any circumstances.

4. Heat ghee in a black iron kadhai or a flat, iron jelabi kadhai. Heat and slowly slide one cake in the hot oil. Keep stirring it lightly in the ghee. It should not stick to the bottom of the vessel. When the lower side is red or light brown turn it over and cook in the same way, shifting it from side to side.

5. Now poke a skewer in the centre of the cake so the ghee rushes within and cooks the centre completely. Use two flat spatulas with holes to lift the cake from the ghee. Allow to drain in a large sieve. Cool and use.

Potli (1)
Gor-Papri (32)
Parsi Poro (63)
Parsi Sev (12)
Vardhvara (37)
Papads (132)
Malido (17)
Boiled eggs

A VISIT TO THE DOCKS AND FORT FISH MARKET

My son Kurush was a great help to me when I was running the Princess Victoria Mary Gymkhana. Hardly was he home from boarding school in Panchgani and in his first year at Wilson College, when he started helping me to shop, especially for fish. He used to go to the Sassoon Docks by 6.30 a.m. and buy fish and prawns sold in auctions. It was a real experience – and a nasty one at that. You got hit in the ribs, pushed and jerked and your fish could be stolen under your nose if you weren't careful. When I used to go in earlier days, I used to wear gum boots, a long skirt and a long sleeved blouse. I remember a – macchan – as we call the fisherwoman — going mad because I'd made a higher bid than her for a kuri (22) pomfrets. She upset the whole basket of fish on the quay and gave me a punch in the chest. But I still feel that this is the best way to get fresh fish at a reasonable price. Today my sons still go to the docks for me, but we also go to Bhau-no-Dhakko or Princes Docks. Ambar or baby shrimps are best bought at the docks. Fresh Bombay Ducks are bought by us, a thousand at a time, the retail market prices too high for us in our business. Crabs, surmai and prawns go in high auctions, especially the large white prawns.

One of the highlights of holiday breakfast for my daughter Freny, was a couple of dozen crisply fried fresh Bombay Ducks with plenty of fresh lime slices.

In our local fish market at Fort, Mumbai, the fisherwomen sit opposite each other on high platforms and shout and screech like call-girls to attract the attention of clients. It's always nice to have your own special macchan who would reduce her price just for you. It became a standard game for the fisher-woman to state a high price for the fish. We had to bid her down by firstly slashing her price to less than 50% of what she had quoted and then bid her lower and lower till she settled for a decent price! And even then we really knew in our heart of hearts, that we had been cheated! Even today I go once a year and buy, especially BHING ROES. It's still a pleasure to see my old friends all heavily jewelled and brightly dressed squabbling over baskets of silver fish.

PAPETA-NE-MACCHI-NA-CUTLES

(Potato Fish Cakes)

Preparation Time: 35 mins.
Cooking Time: 35 mins.   •   Serves 6-8

300 gms. mashed potato
400 gms. fish, boiled and deboned
2   tablespoons coriander seeds, coarsely ground
1   tablespoon cumin seeds, coarsely ground
1   tablespoon black peppercorns, coarsely ground
1   teaspoon chilli powder
1   teaspoon Parsi dhansakh masala
1   teaspoon turmeric powder
2   medium onions finely chopped
3   deseeded green chillies finely chopped
1   cup fresh coriander, washed and finely chopped
1   tablespoon fresh mint, finely chopped
4-6   eggs
2   cups bread crumbs
    salt
    oil

1. Take a large thali or tray and place all the mashed potato and boiled fish on it and mix well.

2. Pick a small vessel or fry pan and place two tablespoons of oil in it. When the oil gets hot, lower the flame and cook all the dry spices for three minutes and tip the mixture over the mashed potato and fish. Add the onions, chillies, coriander, mint and salt and mix all the items thoroughly.

3. Wet your hands and make equal sized balls. Then flatten them and roll the ball in the bread crumbs. Shape the cakes on a wooden board so that they are round and flat at the top and bottom.

4. Beat the eggs. Heat oil in a fry pan and when it starts to smoke lower the flame and dip the cakes in the beaten eggs and fry four at a time till golden brown. Serve with dal or dried vegetables and rotlis.

MACCHI-NA-CUTLES

(Fish Cutlets)

Preparation Time: 36 mins.
Cooking Time: 25 mins.   •   Serves 6-8

2	cups boiled fish or boiled prawns
1	large onion, finely chopped
8	slices of stale bread
1	pod garlic, finely chopped
6	green chillies, finely chopped
$1/2$	cup coriander, finely chopped
2	sour limes, juice removed
1-2	tablespoons sugar
	bread crumbs
4	eggs
2	tablespoons mint, finely chopped
	a pinch of black pepper powder
	salt
	oil

1. Place the fish in a large thali. If using prawns pound them well.

2. Soak the bread in water for five minutes. Squeeze all the water out of the bread between your two hands and place it with the fish in the thali. Chop the onion finely along with washed coriander, mint, green chillies and garlic. Mix well so that the bread and fish are mixed thoroughly. Add the salt, lime juice, pepper powder and sugar. Mix again until you get a smooth mixture.

3. Make equal balls from the mixture, flatten them and form into cutlets. Roll them in bread crumbs.

4. Heat the oil in a fry pan. Beat the eggs in a soup plate. Whisk thoroughly. When the oil is hot, roll the cutlets in the whisked eggs and place a few at a time in the hot oil and fry till golden brown.

5. The number of cutlets will depend upon the size of the fish balls, but, you should get 12-18 cutlets from this mixture.

LAL MASALA BHARELA BANGRA

(Red Chutney Stuffed Mackerel)

Preparation Time: 20 mins.
Cooking Time: 35 mins. • Serves: 8

12	fresh mackerels
1	tablespoon turmeric powder
1	tablespoon red chilli powder
	salt
	oil – preferably til or sesame oil

For the Chutney:

6-10	red dried chillies
2	tablespoons cumin seeds
$1/2$	teaspoon mustard seeds
1	knob of tamarind half the size of a sour lime
1	whole pod of garlic
$1/4$	cup vinegar

1. Grind the chutney masala with salt to taste.

2. Wash and clean the mackerels. Remove the gills and stomach dirt and wash the stomach portion without tearing the fish.

3. Apply salt and mix the fish in the turmeric and chilli powder. Stuff through the gill portion with the chutney.

4. Heat a skillet or tava with sesame oil and fry the fish till golden brown on both sides.

   Serve with rotlis and beans or dal or with vegetable curry and rice.

5. Can also be stuffed with green chutney ground with raw mangoes. It tastes great.

GOVARSING-NE-GHARAB NO-PATIO

(Sweet and sour cluster beans cooked with bhing fish roe – A traditional favourite from Gujarat).

Preparation Time: 45-50 mins.
Cooking Time: 25-30 mins.

2   pairs fresh bhing roes
500 gms. govarsing or cluster beans
1   teaspoon turmeric powder
1/2   kopra, grated
1   tablespoon sesame seeds
1   tablespoon cumin seeds
1   teaspoon black peppercorns
1/2"   piece cinnamon
2   cloves
1   badiyan or star anise
1   whole pod garlic cloves
4   green chillies, deseeded
5   red Kashmiri chillies
1   teaspoon turmeric powder

} To be ground finely in half a cup of vinegar

1   teaspoon chilli powder
1   teaspoon turmeric powder
1/2   cup thick tamarind pulp
1/2   cup jaggery
4   large finely chopped tomatoes
3   large onions
1   sprig curry leaves
1/2   cup coriander, finely chopped
    salt to taste
    oil for cooking

1. Wash the two pairs of fish roes very carefully and separate each of the two parts with a knife. Marinate the fish roe in salt, one teaspoon of turmeric powder and one teaspoon of chilli powder. Set aside in a cool place.

2. Grind the required masala to a fine paste on a stone mortar with half a cup of vinegar.

3. String the govarsing and cut or break into three pieces each. Boil in a pot of salted water and when soft strain through a colander.

4. Place the curry sprigs and chopped onions along with one cup of oil in a large, thick bottomed vessel and cook the onions until soft. Add the ground masala, tomatoes tamarind pulp and jaggery and cook for 10 minutes over a low fire.

5. Meanwhile place an iron skillet or non-stick frying pan onto a stove. Add 1 cup oil and deep fry the 4 large pieces of roe and then cut each piece into 4 portions so that you will have 16 pieces. Fry well until golden brown.

6. To the masala gravy add the boiled govarsing and stir. Spread the vegetable evenly in the pot and place the pieces of fish roe on top. Cover the vessel and gently cook over a low fire. After 10 minutes uncover, turn the roe pieces over and cook for five more minutes. Top with the chopped coriander.

7. Serve with rotlis or parathas.

LILI CHUTNEY BHARELA CHHAMNA

(Pomfret stuffed with green chutney)

Preparation Time: 35-40 mins.
Cooking Time: 40 mins. • Serves 6

No Parsi festival or function is complete without a fish dish on the day's menu. The favourite of children and adults is fried pomfret stuffed with sweet, sour and hot green chutney.

6	small sized whole pomfrets
1	tablespoon turmeric powder
2	tablespoons chilli powder
	oil for frying
	salt to taste

1	fresh coconut, grated	
1	cup coriander leaves	
2	sprigs mint leaves	
5	green chillies	grind till
2	teaspoons cumin seeds	soft in very little water
	teaspoon black peppercorns	
	juice of 2 sour limes	
	tablespoons sugar	
	salt	

1. Grind the coconut masala on a mortar or in a mixer-grinder. I prefer chutneys ground on black stone by pestles.

2. Wash the pomfrets. Keep whole. Slit the side of the face and remove the gills and intestines. Wash thoroughly. Apply salt, turmeric and chilli powder to the pomfrets outside and inside. Stuff the stomach through the gills, with as much chutney as possible.

3. If necessary tie the pomfrets with string so the chutney does not ooze out whilst frying.

4. Take a large tava or skillet and cover the bottom with at least half an inch of oil. Place it on a stove. When the oil is hot place the whole pomfret head first in the oil by the tail. Be careful not to burn your fingers. Take a spoon and pour hot oil over the pomfret. When the pomfrets are well fried on both sides, serve with sour lime pieces.

KARACHLA-NI-KARI

(Crab curry)

Preparation Time: 30 mins.
Cooking Time: 30-35 mins. • Serves 6

10	large crabs	
2	coconuts, thick milk removed	
2	large onions	
16	large Kashmiri chillies	
4	green chillies deseeded	
2	tablespoons cumin seeds	
2	tablespoons garlic cloves, skinned	
50	gms. tamarind	grind
200	gms. red tomatoes, skinned deseeded	finely with half a cup
1"	cinnamon	of water
4	cloves	
12	black peppercorns	
1	teaspoon fresh turmeric, grated	
2	stems curry leaves	
	salt	

1. Clean and cut the crabs carefully. Remove the dead man's fingers. Wash twice, crack each claw once, apply salt and set aside.

2. Remove the thick coconut milk.

3. Grind all the condiments finely with half a cup of water.

4. Take a heavy bottomed pan and place in it the curry leaves, masala and coconut milk and allow to boil. Add the salted crabs, lower flame and allow to cook for half an hour. Taste for salt. Serve with plain boiled white rice.

SOOKKA BOOMLA NO TARAPORI PATIO

(Dried Bombay Duck Pickle)

Preparation Time: 40 mins.
Cooking Time: 35-45 mins.

50	dried Bombay ducks
¼	teacup sugarcane vinegar
25	Kashmiri chillies
3	pods garlic
4	tablespoons cumin seeds
1	tablespoon mustard seed
1	tablespoon black peppercorns
1	cup vinegar
300	gms. jaggery
	salt
	oil

grind together in ¼ cup of vinegar

1. Remove the heads and tails of the Bombay ducks. Cut each into three pieces and clean the stomach cavity. Soak in water for half an hour and clean them well, wash and set aside.

2. Grind the masala by adding the sugarcane vinegar.

3. Take a vessel with a large mouth. Pour in two to three cups of oil. Allow it to heat and add the masala and cook it with the jaggery and one cup of vinegar. When the gravy boils add the washed Bombay duck pieces to it and cook over a gentle flame till soft. If you find that more gravy is necessary add a little more vinegar. Salt to taste.

4. This patia can be preserved for weeks and in the villages of Gujarat, Parsi families used to cook it for their relatives to take to Bombay as a gift. It was also cooked and preserved for the monsoons when no fresh fish was available and eaten with tittori or val-ni-dar.

5. I use it as a pickle with yellow dar or vegetables.

TARELA TAJA BOOMLA

[Fresh Bombay Ducks fried (First Method)]

Preparation Time: 20 mins.
Cooking Time: 30-40 mins. • Serves 6-8

Bombay ducks should be very fresh and pinkish near the mouth and head when you buy them. In our family this fish is traditionally had for breakfast. It is not kept for lunch and dinner. Each person eats six to twelve Bombay ducks with lots of lime juice squeezed on them.

24	Bombay ducks
1	cup wheat flour
2-3	cups gram flour
3-5	tablespoons red chilli powder
2	tablespoons turmeric powder
4	sour limes
	salt
	oil

1. Clean the Bombay ducks by cutting off the heads, fins and tails. Take a sharp knife and scrape off all the dirt and tiny scales. Wash them.

2. Add one cup wheat flour and mix it in the ducks. Roll them between your hands and then wash all the flour off. Wash them in a colander so all the water is strained off. Salt and marinate in the chilli and turmeric powder.

3. Place two frying pans half filled with oil on your gas stoves. On a nearby table spread a newspaper with some gram flour.

4. When the oil is hot, roll the Bombay ducks in the gram flour. See that the ducks are thoroughly coated with the flour, and immerse them one by one, by picking them up from their tailends, in the boiling oil. Fry in small batches and send them to be eaten at the table straight from the pan. The fish should be crisp on the outside.

TARELA TAJA BOOMLA

[Fresh Bombay Ducks fried
(Second Method)]

Preparation Time: 25 mins.
Cooking Time: 30-40 mins. • Serves 6-8

24	Bombay ducks
1	cup wheat flour
3-4	cups gram flour
3-4	tablespoons chilli powder
2	tablespoons turmeric powder
2-3	tablespoons tamarind chutney
$\frac{1}{2}$	cup fresh coriander, chopped
4	green chillies finely chopped
1	teaspoon cumin seeds
1	teaspoon coriander seeds
1	teaspoon black peppercorns
	salt
	oil

grind in 2 tablespoons of water

1. Clean and wash the Bombay ducks as described in the first method and marinate in salt, chilli and turmeric powders, tamarind chutney, coriander and green chillies.

2. Grind the coriander seeds, cumin seeds and peppercorns to a fine paste and apply to the Bombay ducks.

3. Place two frying pans on the stoves. Half fill with oil and heat. When the oil smokes, spread gram flour generously on a newspaper. Roll one duck at a time in the gram flour and deep fry in batches of five till golden brown.

4. Fry small batches at a time and serve immediately with sour lime slices. If you allow the Bombay ducks to get cold they will be ruined.

MAIJI NO TAJA BOOMLA NO RAS

(My Great Grandmother's fresh Bombay Duck gravy)

Preparation Time: 12 mins.
Cooking Time: 15 mins. • Serves 6-8

When the fisherwoman came with her terracotta peni or vessel on her head, she brought along an assortment of fish which included crabs, lobsters, Bombay ducks, mullets, prawns and baby pomfrets. Soonamai used to make her empty the whole lot in large round copper vessel called kathrot. The fish was sorted out by Diwali her kitchen maid. The tiny Bombay ducks were separated and cleaned and cooked for lunch in a non-masala gravy which was white in appearance and tasted good. In Bombay we never cook the ducks in gravy — somehow the taste isn't there. It could be because the food was cooked on a wooden fire and the greens were freshly plucked that it tasted so good.

12	small whole Bombay ducks cleaned, heads, tails and fins removed
2	large onions finely chopped
1	teaspoon cumin seeds, coarsely ground
5	green chillies, finely chopped
$\frac{1}{2}$	bunch fresh coriander, finely chopped
2	sprigs curry leaves
2	tablespoons rice flour
2	tablespoons crushed garlic
	salt
	oil

1. Place onions and half a cup oil in a vessel over a low fire and cook till soft and pink. Add the garlic, cumin seeds, green chillies and curry leaves. Cook for two minutes and add the rice flour. Mix vigorously for two minutes and add three cups of water and allow to boil. Taste for salt.

2. Place the salted Bombay ducks in the boiling gravy for five to seven minutes and remove from the fire. Sprinkle the coriander on top of the gravy.

VALSAD NO LODHI PER NO SUKKA BOOMLA NO PATIO

(Valsad type dried Bombay Ducks cooked on a Griddle)

Preparation Time: 1 hr. 15 mins.
Cooking Time: 35 mins. • Serves 6

15 dried Bombay ducks
2   large onions very finely minced
2   large potatoes very finely chopped
2   teaspoons chilli powder
2   teaspoons turmeric powder
1   teaspoon Parsi dhansakh powder
2   tablespoons garlic crushed
1   tablespoon cumin seeds coarsely ground
1/2 cup tamarind juice
2   teaspoons jaggery
12 curry leaves
    salt
    mustard oil

1. Cut off the heads, fins and tails of the Bombay ducks and soak in water for an hour. When the Bombay ducks softens, tear apart and remove the centre bone and shred the ducks with your fingers. Wash and drain.

2. Mix the onions, potatoes, Bombay ducks, chilli, turmeric, dhansakh powders, garlic, cumin, tamarind juice and jaggery in a clean bowl. Mix well. Add a pinch of salt.

3. Take a very large fish tava, pour one cup mustard oil on it and allow to heat well. Add the curry leaves and then the fish mixture. Lower the flame and mix well non-stop. After five minutes invert a vessel over the mixture and allow to cook on a very low flame in its own steam. Remove vessel, mix and cover again. See that the patia does not stick to the tava and burn.

DEHNU NO LÉVTI-NO-PATIO

(Patia of Mud-Fish)

Preparation Time: 45 mins.
Cooking Time: 40 mins. • Serves 7-8

This is not a fish which is normally available in the Bombay markets. One has to order it from the local fisherwomen. But on the west coast of Gujarat it is very easily available. This fish has to be brought alive. It has to be washed two-three times in wheat flour and its head has to be chopped off as well as its tiny tail. These mud fish are smaller than our fingers. Washing them with wheat flour helps to remove the tiny scales which stick to them.

500 gms. mud fish, cleaned and salted
8   red chillies
4   green chillies   ⎫ grind in
1   tablespoon cumin seeds ⎬ 1/2 cup
1   pod garlic   ⎪ sugarcane
1   teaspoon black peppercorns ⎭ vinegar
2   onions
2   cups sugarcane vinegar
    salt
    oil

1. Grind the masala in strong half cup sugar-cane vinegar.

2. Wash, clean and salt the mud fish and set aside.

3. Chop the onions and fry in half a cup of oil. When soft add the masala and cook it over a slow fire. Add one cup strong vinegar and add the mud fish. Do not stir the fish with a spoon, but shake the vessel from side to side. Add a little more vinegar if it is necessary and cook till soft.

4. Store in a glass vessel in a cool place. It will remain for several days and can be eaten as a pickle.

KESAR-MA-RAMAS-NA-TUKRA

(Salmon fillets cooked in saffron sauce)

Preparation Time: 15-20 mins.
Cooking Time: 20-25 mins. • Serves 6

8	thick rawas fish fillets
1	coconut, milk removed
1	gm. saffron
1	teaspoon chilli powder
1	tablespoons black peppercorns
2	tablespoons garlic, sliced
1	green chilli, finely chopped
1	large onion, finely chopped
1	tablespoon rice flour
2	tablespoons chopped coriander
	mint sprigs
	butter
	salt to taste

1. Wash the fish fillets and marinate in salt and set aside.

2. Heat the saffron and crumble into a cup of hot water and allow to steep. Keep the milk of one coconut in a cool place.

3. Fry the onion in three tablespoons butter. Add the green chilli and garlic slices. Cook till soft. Mix the rice flour in half a cup of water and add it along with the coconut milk and the steeped saffron. Lower the flame and cook for 10 minutes till the gravy thickens. Taste for salt.

4. Take a thick paper bag and place the peppercorns in it and pound with a heavy pestle. Sprinkle the fish with chilli powder and roll in the crushed peppercorns.

5. Heat three or more tablespoons of butter and fry the fish fillets over medium heat till both sides turn brown. Remove on a flat dish.

6. Reheat the saffron coconut gravy, do not boil, pour over fish fillets. Sprinkle the chopped coriander on top, dot with mint and serve with toast.

SOONAMAI–NI–TARELI SONDH

(Soonamai's fried lobsters)

Preparation Time: 1 hr.-15 mins.
Cooking Time: 20-25 mins. • Serves 6

12	baby lobsters with tails deveined with shells on	
2	sour limes	
1/2	tablespoon turmeric powder	
1	tablespoon cumin seeds	grind in the
1	tablespoon sesame seeds	juice of two
4	green chillies, deseeded	sour limes
3	red dried chillies	
6	black peppercorns	
	salt	
	sesame oil for frying	

1. Wash the lobster with tails and marinate them in the masala. Turn them over as many times as you can within the one hour they are kept in the masala.

2. Take a large iron tava and pour half a bottle of sesame oil onto it. Heat the oil well and place the lobsters with tails in rows. Turn once after two minutes and lower flame and cover with a high domed vessel. Allow to cook for 10 minutes over a low fire. Remove the cover, cook for further five minutes and serve at once.

MACCHI–NI–KARI

(Special Prawn or Fish Currry)

Preparation Time: 20-25 mins.
Cooking Time: 35-45 mins. • Serves: 6-8

2-3	cups deveined prawns **or**
10-12	pieces of fish
6	drumsticks
1	coconut milk removed
2	tablespoons kokum
6	green chillies–deseeded and split
1	coconut grated
12-16	Kashmiri chillies
2	tablespoons coriander seeds
1	tablespoon khaskhas
1	tablespoon sesame seeds
1"	piece fresh turmeric
2	large onions, grated
4	large tomatoes, chopped
$1/4$	cup chana or grams
$1/2$	cup cashewnuts
1	whole pod garlic
$1/2$	cup tamarind pulp
2	sprigs curry leaves
	oil
	salt

grind together with water

1. Wash the fish or prawns, apply salt and set aside.
2. Take a large, open mouthed vessel. Pour half a cup or more of oil. Place it on the stove and add the curry leaves to it. When the oil gets hot add all the ground masala, the green chillies and fry well till red. Add any water left over from the masala as well as the coconut milk and stir well. Add salt to taste. If you feel that you will be needing more liquid add one cup of water at a time. Bring to a boil and put in the prawns or fish, lower the flame and allow to simmer for ten minutes for fish and 20 minutes for prawns. Wash kokum and add to the curry.
3. Clean the drumsticks, cut each into three, four or six pieces and cook till tender in salted water. Drain the water and put the drumsticks into the curry along with the tamarind pulp. Cook for a few minutes longer. When in season add one to two raw, peeled mangoes cut into quarters.
4. Serve with boiled basmati rice, onion salad and papads.

TARELI MACCHI

(Fried fish Parsi style)

Preparation Time: 1 hr.-15 mins.
Cooking Time: 20-25 mins. • Serves 6

1	large pomfret cut into 4-6 slices
1-2	teaspoons chilli powder
1	teaspoon turmeric powder
$1/2$	teaspoon coriander seed powder
$1/2$	teaspoon black pepper powder
	salt to taste
	oil as required

1. Wash fish well, apply salt, the masala powders and allow to marinate for half an hour.
2. Take a large non-stick pan or a round tava. Pour oil on it and put it on the fire.
3. When the oil is hot, fry the fish but do not allow it to harden. Serve with lemon wedges and green chutney.

BAPAIJI NO KOLMI-NO-PATIO

(Grandmother's Prawn Patio)

Preparation Time: 15 mins.
Cooking Time: 25-35 mins. • Serves: 4-6

This is a great delicacy for sea-food lovers and will keep for a week if cooked only in vinegar and without the addition of onions and tomatoes.

2	cups shelled deveined prawns	
10-12	Kashmiri chillies deseeded	
1	large pod garlic	ground in
1	tablespoon cumin seeds	half cup vinegar
1/2	teaspoon mustard seeds	
1	teaspoon peppercorns	
1	tablespoon dhansakh masala	
3	large onions finely chopped	
10	cherry tomatoes	
2	capsicums cut into small squares	
1/2	teaspoon turmeric powder	
	curry leaves	
50	gms. jaggery	

1. Grind all the masalas to a soft consistency using as much vinegar as necessary.

2. Fry the chopped onion in half a cup of oil till golden. Add the ground masala, turmeric, dhansakh masala, curry leaves and cook it over a low flame. Add the prawns and fry in the masala. When it becomes dry add the jaggery, any remaining vinegar, the cherry tomatoes, capsicums and one cup water. Simmer till cooked. Sprinkle fresh coriander and serve with parathas or the famous Parsi Dhan-Dar or white rice and yellow dal.

PIROJA'S KHATTI-MITTHI-BOI

(Piroja's Mullets in hot sour gravy)

Preparation Time: 15-20 mins.
Cooking Time: 20-25 mins. • Serves: 4

6	mullets, about 6" long	
1	coconut milk removed	
2	brinjals	
8	Kashmiri chillies	
2"	piece of ginger	
2	large onions	grind
3	large tomatoes	fine
1	tablespoon khaskhas	
2	tablespoons gram	
1/2	cup tamarind water	
	curry leaves	
	salt	
5	tablespoons sesame oil	

1. Clean and wash the mullets. Remove gills and entrails. Leave the fish intact. Wash twice, apply salt and keep aside. Skin the brinjals and cut into large pieces.

2. Grate the coconut and after grinding it squeeze out the milk with the help of hot water. Do this twice.

3. Grind together the chillies, ginger, khaskhas or poppy seeds, gram, tomatoes and onions.

4. Heat the oil. Drop in the curry leaves and the ground masala and stir till red hot. Pour in the coconut milk which should consist of at least four cups. Add the brinjals. Cook for 10 minutes. Add the whole mullets. Bring to the boil. Add the tamarind water and simmer for five to seven minutes.

Serve with yellow rice and papad.

KOLMI-NA-KABAB

(Prawn Kababs)

Preparation Time: 10 mins.
Cooking Time: 20 mins. • Serves: 4-6

2	cups prawns shelled, deveined, coarsely ground	
1	medium sized onion	
2	eggs, beaten	
2	large boiled potatoes	
1	tablespoon cumin seeds	
10	black peppercorns	grind
6	green chillies, deseeded	fine
1	teaspoon poppy seeds	
8-10	cloves garlic	
	juice of one lemon	
1/4	bunch coriander, washed and chopped	
1/2	cup breadcrumbs/flour	
	salt to taste	
	sweet oil for frying	

1. Grind finely cumin, garlic, green chillies, peppercorns, poppy seeds and boiled potatoes into a firm paste without using any water. Add coarsely ground prawns to it. Salt to taste. Mix well.

2. Chop the onion very fine. Mix together the stiffly beaten eggs, juice of one lemon, onion and chopped coriander. Fold this into the ground prawn mixture. Mix thoroughly and divide into little round balls. Coat with breadcrumbs or any other flour and deep fry in hot oil. Take care not to fry too many at one time.

3. Serve with masala dal and rice or with drinks or any vegetable dish.

4. Wet your hands whilst making the balls to get a smooth external covering before coating with the bread crumbs.

SASUJI NO AMBAR-NO-LODHI-PER-NO-PATIO

(Mother-in-law's Shrimps cooked on an Iron Skillet)

Preparation Time: 10 mins.
Cooking Time: 25-30 mins. • Serves: 4-6

3	cups shelled ambar or baby shrimps	
3	cups onions, finely chopped	
1	cup raw mangoes, finely chopped	
4	teaspoons green chillies, finely chopped	
1/2	cup fresh coriander, finely chopped	
1/2	teaspoon black peppercorns	
2	tablespoons cumin seeds	
1	teaspoon mustard seeds	Grind together
2	tablespoons garlic cloves	with a quarter
1	tablespoon Parsi dhansakh masala	cup of water
1/2	tablespoon turmeric powder	
1/2	teaspoon fennel seeds	
1	tablespoon fresh mint, finely chopped	
	salt	
	mustard oil	

1. Place one cup of mustard oil on a large tava. Allow to heat and add the onions. Stir with a spatula till cooked and golden brown. Add the ground masala and fry till red. Once the masala is fried, add the salted ambar and lower the flame and cook till soft. Stir frequently.

2. When the ambar is soft add the raw chopped mangoes, green chillies and the coriander. Keep the tava on a very slow fire. Keep stirring till the mango pieces soften and are well blended with the ambar and onions. Taste for salt. Serve sprinkled with fresh mint and eat it with hot khichri or rotlis.

VENGHNA-MA-AMBAR

(Shrimps cooked with Brinjals)

Preparation Time: 12 mins.
Cooking Time: 25-30 mins. • Serves: 4

2	medium sized brinjals, peeled
2	bunches spring onions
2	green chillies
1	cup shrimps or ambar, shelled
$^1/_4$	cup fresh coriander, chopped
$^1/_2$	cup spinach
$^1/_2$	teaspoon turmeric powder
1	heaped tablespoon ginger-garlic paste
$^1/_4$	teaspoon oregano
	oil
	salt to taste

1. Cut the brinjals into tiny pieces and soak in salted water. Finely chop the spring onions and spinach.

2. Place the onions in a kadhai with half a cup oil. When cooked and transparent add oregano, the ginger-garlic paste, salt and the brinjal pieces. Throw away the salt water. Cover and cook over a low fire. When the brinjals are half-cooked add the shrimps, turmeric powder, spinach and green chillies. Cover and allow the brinjals to become soft and tender. When the brinjal is soft and mushy, mix well and add the fresh coriander.

3. Serve with lemon wedges and hot parathas.

4. If available, use one chopped green mango, whilst cooking the brinjal and shrimps.

SOONAMAI-NI-MALAI-MA KOLMI

(Soonamai's Prawns)

Preparation Time: 12 mins.
Cooking Time: 25-30 mins. • Serves: 6-8

500 gms.	large prawns, shelled, deveined	
200 gms.	fresh cream or malai	
100 gms.	cashewnuts	Grind together
6	large Kashmiri chillies	Grind together
6	black peppercorns	Grind together
3	green chillies, slit	
$^1/_2$	teaspoon shahjeera	
$^1/_2$	cup coriander washed, chopped	
1	large onion chopped	
	salt	
$^1/_2$	cup oil	

1. Apply salt on the washed prawns. Grind the cashewnuts, red chillies and black peppercorns to a smooth paste and mix the prawns in it.

2. Heat the oil and when it starts smoking, lower flame and add the onions, slit chillies and shahjeera. Lower the flame further and drop the prawns into the pan and stir carefully so that all the prawns get cooked. Cover with a lid, add 3 tablespoons of water and cook over a low fire till prawns are soft and tender. If necessary add some more water. Taste for salt.

3. Mix the cream, add a pinch of salt and pour over the cooked prawns. Stir, bring to a gentle boil and remove from the fire. Sprinkle the coriander over the prawns and serve.

SOONAMAI-NI-KOLMI-NE-PAPETA-NO-VAGHAR

(Soonamai's Prawn and Potato Salnu)

Preparation Time: 15 mins.
Cooking Time: 20-30 mins. • Serves: 6

2   cups prawns, deveined washed
3   large potatoes skinned and cubed
2   large onions finely chopped
8   green chillies
20 gms. skinned garlic ⎱ grind
20 gms. cumin seeds   ⎰ together
10 gms. fennel seeds
1   teaspoon turmeric powder
2   tablespoons roasted coarsely ground sesame seeds
1/4 bunch coriander leaves washed and finely chopped
1   sprig curry leaves
    salt
    oil

1. Place the onions and half cup oil in a pan and cook over a medium flame till pink. Add the potatoes and cover the pan and simmer over a low fire for five minutes. Add prawns, half a cup of water and salt to taste, mix, cover and cook for 10 minutes. Add the curry leaves, turmeric, ground masala and the sesame seeds. Mix and cook for a further 10 minutes covered till potatoes and prawns are tender. If necessary add half a cup of water. The potatoes must be soft to the touch. Garnish with coriander.

2. Serve with plenty of sour lime and rotlis.

KOLMI-NA-BHAJIA

(Prawn Bhajias or Batter Fried Prawns)

Preparation Time: 10 mins.
Cooking Time: 20-25 mins. • Serves: 6-8

2   cups fresh prawns, deveined
1 1/2 cups gram flour
1   large onion finely chopped
6   green chillies finely chopped
1/2 cup fresh coriander finely chopped
2   tablespoons mint finely chopped
2   teaspoons red chilli powder
1   teaspoon turmeric powder
1   teaspoon Parsi dhansakh masala
1   pinch cooking soda
2   sour limes juice only
1   tablespoon sugar
    salt
    oil

1. Mash the prawns with a sharp knife, apply salt and place in a thali. Add all the ingredients and salt to taste and mix well with half a cup of water. Make a nice soft dough and roll into little balls with wet hands. If mixture is too tight add a little more water.

2. Place oil in a kadhai and when hot drop in 10 to 15 balls at a time. Fry till red and drain in a colander.

3. Serve with green coconut or tamarind chutney.

SOONAMAI-NO-KOLMI-NE-KERA-NI-CHAAL-NO-RAS

(Soonamai's Prawn and Banana Skin Curry)

Preparation Time: 25 mins.
Cooking Time: 35 mins. • Serves: 6-8

45   medium sized prawns, washed
     and deveined
6   green banana skins, washed
1   large onion ⎫
6   Kashmiri chillies
1"   piece cinnamon
3   mace flowers
2   green cardamoms ⎬ grind well
12   cloves garlic
10   black peppercorns
¼   teaspoon poppy seeds
2   tablespoons coriander,
     chopped ⎭
2   cups coconut milk
1   sour lime, juice removed
1   sprig curry leaves
1   tablespoon sugar
     salt
     sesame oil

1. Chop the banana skin into 1" pieces and place in a sauce pan of water. Add half a teaspoon of salt and cook till soft. The pieces should be intact.

2. Grind all the spices including the onion and coriander to a soft paste with a little water.

3. Heat half a cup of sesame oil. Add the curry leaves and toss in the ground masala. Lower heat and stir till red. Add the washed prawns and lower the heat and cook for five minutes. Add two cups of coconut milk and the banana skins and allow to simmer for 20 minutes. Taste for salt, add sugar and lime juice and remove from the fire. Serve with rice and papads.

KOLMI-NE-KOTHMIR-MA-PANEER

(Casserole of prawns and cottage cheese)

Preparation Time: 20 mins.
Cooking Time: 40 mins. • Serves 6

2   cups large prawns, deveined and salted
300 gms. punjabi paneer
½   bunch fresh coriander
2   large onions, chopped finely
2   tablespoons green chillies, finely chopped
½   cup butter
¼   teaspoon ajma seeds or oregano
½   teaspoon mustard seeds
½   teaspoon carraway seeds
2   teaspoons chilli powder
½   cup tomato pulp
2   sprigs curry leaves
7   peppercorns coarsely ground
     salt to taste
3   tablespoons butter

1. Heat three tablespoons butter in a heavy bottomed pan. Add the chopped onions and cook until soft. Add the curry leaves, carraway, ajma, mustard seeds and allow them to pop. Quickly toss in the powdered spices, green chillies, finely pulped tomatoes and prawns. Turn the heat low and allow to simmer for 15-20 minutes adding half a cup water if necessary till the prawns are tender. Add the chopped coriander.

2. Cut the paneer into bite size cubes. Heat a frying pan half full with oil. When the oil is hot gently slide in the paneer cubes in two batches. Remove with a slotted spoon when golden brown and immediately put it in the cooked prawn mixture. Stir well.

3. Place the prawn and paneer mixture onto a heated dish and serve immediately with hot rotlis or yellow rice.

KOLMI-NE-LAL KOHRA-NO-SAAK

(Red Pumpkin and Prawn Casserole)

Preparation Time: 15 mins.
Cooking Time: 25 mins. • Serves 8-10

2   cups prawns, deveined
1   kg. red pumpkin
250 gms. ripe tomatoes
4   green chillies, deseeded
2   tablespoons coriander, chopped
2   sprigs curry leaves
1¹/₂"ginger
1   teaspoon cumin seeds, coarsely ground
¹/₂   teaspoon turmeric powder
3   teaspoons chilli powder
¹/₄   teaspoon mustard seeds
¹/₂   sour lime, juice only
2   teaspoons sugar
3   tablespoons ghee

1. Peel the pumpkin, cut into large square pieces and boil in four cups of water. Cook until soft and grind to a soft smooth pulp through a sieve or moulee legume.

2. Chop the green chillies and ginger finely. Peel the tomatoes and cut into small pieces.

3. Heat the ghee in a flat shallow pan and add the mustard seeds and curry leaves. Allow to splutter; then lower heat and add green chillies, ginger, cumin seeds, turmeric and chilli powder. Stir, add the tomatoes and prawns and then cover and allow to cook over a low fire for at least 5-10 minutes after which the pumpkin pulp should be added. Cover and cook for another 10 minutes. Salt to taste.

4. Just before serving add the juice of half a sour lime and two teaspoons sugar. Sprinkle with chopped coriander and serve.

MASALA-NI-KOLMI

(Prawns cooked in hot gravy)

Preparation Time: 20 mins.
Cooking Time: 40 mins. • Serves 6

2   cups large prawns, deveined and salted
4   large tomatoes
1   pod garlic ⎫
2   teaspoons cumin seeds ⎬ grind together
6-8 dried Kashmiri chillies ⎭
2   teaspoons Parsi dhansakh masala powder
4   large onions
2   sprigs curry leaves
1   cup coriander leaves
       salt to taste
       refined oil

1. Grind the garlic, cumin seeds and red chillies to a fine paste in your mixer grinder or on a stone pestle with a little water.

2. Chop the onions and place them in a dekchi with the curry leaves and one cup of refined oil. When the onions are placed on the stove allow them to become pink and soft, then lower the flame and add the ground and the powdered masala. Stir vigorously till a lovely aroma arises from the pan. Then skin and deseed the tomatoes. Chop finely and add to the pan.

3. When the tomatoes soften up, add the washed salted prawns and the coriander. Cook over a slow flame without water till prawns are tender and soft. If by any chance your gravy sticks to the bottom because you have not lowered the flame sufficiently, add 1/2 cup water.

Kharoo Gos   (76
Bhunjeli-Gos-Ni-Tang (75
Mutton No Bafaat   (79

SOONAMAI NA BHIDA-MA-KOLMI

(Lady-fingers cooked with Prawns)

Preparation Time: 15 mins.
Cooking Time: 30-35 mins. • Serves 4-6

300 gms. lady fingers
1 cup prawns, deveined
2 onions, finely chopped
2 tomatoes, finely chopped
1 cup coriander leaves
2 tablespoons mint, chopped
1 teaspoon chilli powder
1 teaspoon amchur powder
1 teaspoon turmeric powder
$\frac{1}{2}$ teaspoon cumin seeds, ground
1 teaspoon sesame seeds
$\frac{1}{2}$ teaspoon mustard seeds
  oil
  salt

1 Wash the prawns, apply salt and set aside. Wash and dry the lady-fingers and cut into slices, a quarter of an inch thick.

2. Place half a cup of oil in a fry pan and cook the onions in it till pink and soft. Add the chilli and turmeric powders, cumin, sesame and mustard seeds. Stir well and add the prawns. Cover and cook for a few minutes. Add half a cup of water, coriander, tomatoes and mint. Cover and cook till the prawns soften.

3. Put oil in a separate fry pan. Apply salt to the lady-fingers and deep fry. Drain. Cover the cooked prawns with the lady-fingers, amchur powder and allow to simmer for five minutes. Mix before serving.

Marghi Na Farchas   (3)
Lal Rajma Ni Dar   (116)
Karachla Ni Kari   (41)

KACCHI-KERI-AMBAR-MA-RANDHELI

(Raw mangoes cooked with baby shrimps)

Preparation Time: 15 mins.
Cooking Time: 25 mins. • Serves 6

2 cups baby shrimps, shelled
2 large onions, finely chopped
2 medium sized raw mangoes, finely chopped
4 green chillies, deseeded and chopped
$\frac{1}{2}$ cup coriander, chopped
1 tablespoon fresh mint, finely chopped
1 tablespoon Parsi dhansakh masala
1 teaspoon turmeric powder
2 teaspoons sugar
1 green lettuce
  oil
  salt

1. For this dish it would be best to cook the baby shrimps on a large iron tava on which we Indians cook our rotlis. If you don't have an iron tava use an iron frying pan. If you don't have one, then use whatever sort of frying pan you possess.

2. Place the finely chopped onions with half a cup of oil on the stove. Cook the onions till golden brown, add the raw mangoes, chillies and the baby shrimps after washing them twice and draining them from a colander. If necessary add some more oil and fry the shrimps and cook without any water. When the shrimps are half done add the powdered spices, sugar, salt, the mint and coriander. Keep stirring the shrimps and cook over a slow fire so that the natural juice of the shrimps does not evaporate totally.

3. When the shrimps are cooked, serve them on a bed of lettuce leaves in a glass dish.

CHEESE LAGARELA FILLET TAMOTA NA SAUCE SATHE

(Crumb fried cheese fish fillets with hot tomato sauce)

Preparation Time: 20 mins.
Cooking Time: 35 mins. • Serves 4-6

1   kg. ripe tomatoes, skinned, deseeded, pureed
2   large pomfrets, filleted
2   sour limes, juice removed
2   teaspoons black pepper powder
2   cups grated cheese
1   bunch parsley
2   beetroots boiled, sliced
2   lettuce, washed
2   cucumbers, skinned and sliced
2   cups toasted bread crumbs
1   onion sliced
4   eggs whisked
1   tablespoon freshly chopped mint
1   teaspoon cornflour
    salt to taste
    oil for deep frying

1. Wash the fillets and marinate in salt, lime juice and black pepper powder.

2. Whisk eggs well along with the cornflour in a soup plate.

3. Heat 4 cups of oil in a large kadhai or fry pan.

4. Roll the grated cheese on the inner side of the fish. Dip the fillets in the egg mixture and coat with bread crumbs and deep fry 3-4 at a time according to the size of the kadhai. Remove from the oil when golden brown. Tie 3 sprigs of parsley in bunches and also deep fry.

5. Arrange the fish fillets on a flat dish covered with lettuce and surrounded by rings of onions, cucumber, beetroot and lemon wedges.

For the hot Tomato Sauce:
1   cup tomato ketchup
1   tablespoon tobasco or capsico sauce
1   teaspoon sugar
1   tablespoon cornflour

Place the fresh tomato puree in a saucepan along with the mint. Add one cup tomato ketchup, one tablespoon tobasco or capsico sauce, one teaspoon sugar and one tablespoon cornflour mixed in three tablespoons water. Stir over a high flame and bring to a fast boil. Taste for salt. Serve along with fillets. Takes 10-12 minutes to make.

TARELI KOLMI

(Parsi Fried Prawns)

Preparation Time: 1 hour
Cooking Time: 20-25 mins. • Serves 6

20   large prawns, shelled and deveined
3   teaspoons chilli powder
2   teaspoons turmeric powder
$1/2$ teaspoon coriander seed powder
$1/2$ teaspoon black pepper powder
     salt to taste
     oil as required

1. Wash the prawns well, apply salt, add the masalas and allow to marinate for half an hour.

2. Take a large non-stick pan or a round tava. Place oil on it and put it on the fire.

3. When the oil is hot, fry the prawns but do not allow them to harden and become plastiky. Cover and cook. Serve with lemon wedges and green chutney.

MACCHI NA FILLET TARTARE SAUCE NI SATHE

(Frilled Fillets with Tartare Sauce)

Preparation Time: 30-45 mins.
Cooking Time: 20-25 mins. • Serves 4-6

For the Fillets:
2	large pomfrets, each cut into fillets
2	sour limes, juice removed
1	teaspoon black pepper powder
1	teaspoon red chilli powder
$\frac{1}{2}$	cup toasted sesame seeds, coarsely crushed
2-3	cups toasted bread crumbs
6	eggs whisked
1	tablespoon cornflour
	salt
	oil

For the Tartare & sauce: Finely Mince Ingredients by Knife
$\frac{1}{2}$	cup chives, chopped
$\frac{1}{2}$	cup spring onions, chopped
$\frac{1}{2}$	cup cucumber, minced (seed portion omitted)
2	tablespoons parsley, minced
2	tablespoons celery, minced
2	tablespoons gherkins, minced
2	tablespoons capsicum, minced
2	cups mayonnaise
1	cup tomato ketchup
1	tablespoon tobasco or capsico sauce
	salt/pepper

1. Place all the minced and chopped vegetables in a rounded glass bowl. Add the ketchup, mayonnaise and tobasco sauce. Taste for salt. Stir gently. Cover with foil and chill.

2. Wash the fillets, you should get 8 large or 16 small ones. Marinate for half an hour in salt, chilli powder, pepper and lime juice.

3. Whisk the eggs in a bowl along with the cornflour.

4. Mix the bread crumbs and seasame seeds. Heat oil in a large kadhai or fry pan. When the oil starts smoking, lower the heat a little and roll the fillets in the bread crumbs and sesame seeds. Dip in the egg and deep fry 2-3 at a time. If the oil is scorching, the fillets will become dark coloured. So raise and lower heat as needed.

5. Lay a dark green banana leaf on a silver salver and stack the fillets neatly one upon the other.

To decorate:

1 sliced fresh pineapple — with skin. Diagonally chopped spring onions and carrots julienne and tomato wedges.

6. Surround the fish fillets with pineapple slices. Scatter the carrots and spring onion over the fish. Alternately you can serve it with tomato wedges or sliced papayas. Serve with the chilled sauce.

PARTY RECIPE

(Fish au Gratin)

Preparation Time: 25 mins
Cooking Time: about 1 hour • Serves 6

The Parsis got on well with their British rulers, they adopted many of their customs, their mode of dress and even their food habits. Since they entertained each other, Parsis soon started having English food items at their tables. They kept butlers who wore spick and span white uniforms and served meals wearing long white gloves. When many Parsi boys were sent abroad to England for their education they had to adapt to the climate and tablefare or starve. So whilst most people in India don't eat beef, pork, bacon and sausages, many Parsis eat all these items.

A really heavy breakfast on Sundays would consist of porridge, mince, kidneys, liver or sausages, and a variety of egg dishes as well as cream, butter, jam and marmalade.

Since the Parsis love fish, various types of baked fish dishes became very popular. The pomfret is very much loved by the community, fried, steamed or baked and was a must at all important gatherings. This particular baked dish was a favourite of my family, even the vegetarians.

8	fillets from 2 large pomfrets
2	sour limes juice removed
$1/2$	cup parsley, finely chopped
$1/2$	cup chives, cut finely
500 gms.	potatoes cooked and mashed
2	cups grated cheese
2	large tomatoes skinned, deseeded and made into pulp
1	litre milk
4	tablespoons maida or self raising flour
1	cup butter
2	tablespoons black pepper, coarsely ground
$1/2$	teaspoon chilli powder
2	spring onions
	Salt to taste

1. Wash the fish fillets, apply salt and pour the lime juice over them and allow to marinate for 12 minutes.

2. Chop the spring onions in thin small rings.

3. Place the fillets in a flat pan and cover with the spring onions, tomatoes and the chopped parsley and chives. Add 2 cups water and cook till fish is soft. Reserve the fish soup. Strain it. This should take 10 minutes or so.

4. Place the butter and flour in the pan and stir vigorously. Add the pepper, the milk, half litre of the reserved fish soup and make a creamy white sauce. Add half the cheese and stir.

5. Lay the fish in the centre of a baking dish and pour the sauce over it. Pipe the mashed potato all round the dish and sprinkle a little chilli powder.

6. Sprinkle the remainder of the grated cheese on top of the sauce so a thick red crust forms when the dish is baked at 350°F in the oven. Make sure the oven is hot when you place the dish inside it. This will take 35-45 minutes.

7. Serve with toasted triangles of bread and a green salad.

CHICKEN

As far as the Parsis are concerned, they are fond of eating chicken, duck, turkey and various wildfowl such as quails and guineafowl.

My grandmother Soonamai had between eighty to one hundred and twenty chickens roaming all over her yard. There was a large tamarind tree close to the chicken coop. A long narrow ladder stood against the tree and the chickens would climb up the ladder and on to the leafy branches. They would remain there the whole day and at sunset they would flutter down to the ground.

When unexpected guests dropped in, all we had to do was to send a young servant boy to chase and catch two or three hens. My grandfather 'Bawaji' as he was lovingly called, performed the ritual. Homegrown chickens have a delightful flavour unlike todays broillers which we buy in the market. Sometimes when a chicken was cut, we would find a fully developed egg in its womb or several small egg yolks.

Chicken can be eaten boiled, roasted, fried, cooked in masala, cooked boneless, minced and stuffed. What I like best is the dry roasted chicken cooked in salt and ginger-garlic paste, which we brought to Bombay along with fried potatoes or chips.

A few days before we returned to Bombay, my grandmother would send messages to all the nearby villages where chickens were kept, that she needed eggs. So whosoever wanted a little cash would come and sell their eggs to her which were collected, packed in terracotta "matkas" amidst paddy husk and brought to Bombay.

KAJU-NI-MARGHI

(Boneless Chicken cooked in Cashew nut gravy)

Preparation Time: 20 mins.
Cooking Time: 30-35 mins. • Serves 4-5

8	chicken breasts, boneless – cut into 3 pieces each
2	capsicums, sliced
4	potatoes, sliced thick
1	teaspoon ginger-garlic paste
2	large onions, finely chopped
3	bay leaves
4	whole cloves
10	black peppercorns
4	green cardamoms, coarsely pounded
2	one inch pieces cinnamon
1	teaspoon fennel seeds
2	teaspoons cumin seeds
100 gms.	cashewnuts
6	green chillies
1	coconut, milk removed
	salt
1/2	cup oil for chicken
	oil for frying potatoes and capsicums

grind together

1. Wash the chicken pieces and marinate in salt and ginger-garlic paste.

2. Chop the onions and place in a flat bottomed vessel along with half a cup of oil. Cook the onions till soft and add the whole spices and chicken. Cover and allow to cook over a low fire for ten minutes. Let the chicken roast in its own juices. Add the ground masala and fry for five minutes. Cook for seven more minutes and add the coconut milk. Stir, and cook till the chicken is tender and the gravy becomes thick. Taste for salt.

3. Apply salt to the potato slices and fry them till soft and golden. Remove from the oil and fry the capsicum slices for one minute.

4. Serve the chicken on a flat dish and top with the fried potatoes and capsicums.

FRENY-NI-MAKHAN-MA-RANDHELI-AAKHI-MARGHI

(Roast Chicken Freny Style)

Preparation Time: 30-40 mins.
Cooking Time: 45 mins.-1 hr. depending on
Chicken • Serves 6-8

2	small chickens 1 kg. each
400 gms	butter-frozen
1	tablespoon ginger-garlic paste
1	tablespoon fresh black pepper powder
6	large potatoes
4	carrot
8	tiny onions
1	tablespoon tobasco sauce
1	tablespoon cornflour
$1/4$	packet sage
	oil or extra butter

1. Wash the chickens inside and out twice. Tie the legs together. Loosen the skin from the neck portion, cut off neck and insert small slices of frozen butter between the skin and the flesh as far as you can. Apply salt and pepper on the chickens and smear them with the ginger-garlic paste. Place one teaspoon sage in the stomach cavity. Then take a large needle and strong white thread and close up the neck cavity. Smear the chickens from outside with extra butter or oil.

2. Skin and halve the potatoes, slit the carrots into sticks after skinning them. Wash, apply salt and set aside. Skin the onions and keep whole.

3. Take a pyrex dish and set both the chickens in the centre of the dish. Surround the chickens with the potatoes, carrots and onions.

4. Pour one cup of water in the dish and place in the oven at 350°F. Cook till the chickens have browned and are tender. Keep adding a little water as and when required.

5. Remove the chickens and vegetables onto another dish and keep warm. Scrape the juices from the dish and set aside in a bowl.

6. Take a small sauce pan, place a dollop of butter on it along with one tablespoon of cornflour. Stir well and allow to brown. Add the juice from the bowl and stir vigorously. Add salt, black pepper powder to taste or a dash of tobasco sauce and a tablespoon of chopped parsley.

7. Serve the sauce separately in a gravy boat along with green salad and skinned citrus fruit. Serve French bread – it will be the right accompaniment to the tender soft chickens.

ALETI-PALETI

(Chicken Liver Gravy with Gizzards)

Preparation Time: 20 mins
Cooking Time: 30-35 mins. • Serves 6-8

28	chicken livers
10	gizzards
250 gms.	potatoes skinned and cubed
200 gms.	large onions
200 gms.	large tomatoes
25 gms.	jaggery, crushed
13	Kashmiri chillies
2	tablespoon garam masala No. 2 (see page 132)
2	small onions chopped
1	tablespoon ginger-garlic paste
	salt
	ghee

} grind in vinegar

1. Grind the masala in vinegar. Clean and skin the gizzards, wash and cut into small pieces. Apply salt and set aside. Clean the livers and cut each into two pieces. Wash, salt and set aside.

2. Cook the gizzards in a pressure cooker with two cups of water till soft. Drain the gizzards.

3. Heat half a cup of ghee in a pan and put in the masala and cook over a medium flame for five minutes. Add the cooked gizzards and one cup of water and allow to simmer for 10 minutes. Add the crushed jaggery, shake the pan from side to side and remove from the heat.

4. Place one cup ghee in a kadhai and lightly fry the salted livers in small batches till cooked and drop them in the gizzard gravy.

5. Cut onions, potatoes and tomatoes into thick rings. Wash, salt and deep fry the first two. Lay out the gizzard and liver gravy in a flat dish and top with golden fried potato rounds, onion rings and tomato slices.

LILA-MARI-NI-KESARI-MARGHI

(Green Pepper Chicken in Saffron Sauce)

Preparation Time: 10 mins.
Cooking Time: 35-40 mins. • Serves 8

8	chicken breasts, filleted
1	teaspoon ground pepper
2 gms.	saffron
1	sour lime, juice removed
1/2	teaspoon coriander powder
1/2	teaspoon nutmeg powder
1/2	teaspoon mace powder
2	tablespoons cornflour
	butter
1	teaspoon green pickled peppercorns (optional)

1. Wash the filleted breasts and cut each into three strips. Salt and marinate in the lime juice and black pepper and set aside.

2. Half an hour before serving the meal, boil the cut chicken in two cups of water. When the chicken is tender, drain the soup and set it aside to make the gravy.

3. Heat the saffron over a skillet and when crisp powder it over half a cup of warm water.

4. Place 3 tablespoons of butter in a heavy based frying pan over medium heat and add the dried spices and the chicken and allow to simmer over a very low fire.

5. Take another saucepan and add two tablespoons of butter. Add the cornflour and mix vigorously. Then add the saffron water and two cups of chicken soup. Keep stirring the sauce non-stop till you achieve a smooth glossy sauce. If using the green peppercorns add them now. Taste for salt.

6. Take a long, flat dish and place the warm chicken pieces on it. Pour the saffron sauce carefully over them. Serve at once.

MASALA-PECHDAR-MARGHI

(Tasty Chicken Masala)

Preparation Time: 25 mins.
Cooking Time: 35-40 mins. • Serves 6

1½ kgs. chicken cut into
   small pieces
1   gm. saffron
2   large onions chopped finely ⎫
4   green chillies
4   red chillies
4   green cardmom seeds
1" cinnamon piece
6   cloves
20 black peppercorns   ⎬ grind
1   tablespoon ginger, chopped   finely
1   tablespoon garlic, chopped
2   tablespoons mint chopped
½   cup fresh coriander, chopped
1   teaspoon black cumin
    or shahjeera
1   teaspoon black mustard seeds ⎭
    milk of one coconut
    salt
    ghee

1. Wash the chicken pieces well. Discard the neck and fine bones near the breast. Marinate in salt and set aside.

2. Broil the saffron on an iron skillet and crumble it into a cup of hot water.

3. Grind the whole long masala list with half a cup of water till it is very soft.

4. Heat three tablespoons ghee in a large vessel over medium flame. Drop in the chicken pieces and fry till red. Lower the flame, cover and allow the chicken to roast in its own juices for seven minutes. Add the ground masala and stir non-stop for 10 minutes. Add the coconut milk and saffron, taste for salt and place on a low flame for 15 minutes. Serve with rice and papads.

MARGHI-NO-KHURMO

(Chicken Khurma)

Preparation Time: 20-22 mins.
Cooking Time: 30-40 mins. • Serves 8

2   medium sized chickens
15 tiny potatoes
2   gms. saffron
12 Kashmiri chillies
7   cloves
4   cardamoms
1" piece of cinnamon   ⎫ finely
1   teaspoon roasted coriander   ground
    seeds   ⎬ with
1   teaspoon mace   water
1   teaspoon cumin seeds
2   star anise   ⎭
1   teaspoon black peppercorns
1   teaspoon turmeric powder
2   cups fresh tomato pulp
4   large onions finely chopped
1   cup whipped yoghurt
    salt
    oil — preferably fresh white butter

1. Cut each chicken into eight pieces. Discard neck, ribs and wings. Wash well, apply salt and set aside. Heat saffron and steep it in a cup of warm water.

2. Chop the onions and allow to heat in half cup oil or butter. Add the ground spices and toss in the chicken pieces. Mix well. Cook for ten minutes on a slow fire. Add tomato pulp and allow chicken to simmer for seven minutes. Add two cups water and allow the chicken to soften. Add more water only if necessary. Cook till most of the gravy has dried.

3. Skin, salt and deep fry the potatoes whole.

4. When the chicken is soft add the yoghurt and saffron water. Allow the chicken to simmer till the gravy thickens. Stir well. Add the fried potatoes and serve hot with green pea pulao.

DILKHUSH MARGHI

(Chicken Delight)

Preparation Time: 25 mins.
Cooking Time: 35-40 mins. • Serves 8

2 chickens 800 gms. each cut into small pieces.
300 gms. thick yoghurt
500 gms. boiled green peas
1 gm. saffron
3 large onions finely chopped
3 large tomatoes skinned and pulped
4 large bay leaves
4 green cardamoms crushed
1 tablespoon ginger-garlic paste
1" cinnamon
6 cloves
20 black peppercorns
4 flowers of mace
$\frac{1}{2}$ a nutmeg
2 star anise
1 tablespoon fennel seeds
   roasted
1 tablespoon coriander seeds
   roasted
$\frac{1}{2}$ cup finely chopped fresh
   coriander
$1\frac{1}{2}$ teaspoons powdered turmeric
2 teaspoons red chilli powder
   salt
   ghee

} grind finely

1. Wash the chicken pieces, discard bony portions and marinate in salt and ginger-garlic paste and set aside. Warm the saffron and allow it to steep in a cup of hot water.

2. Chop the onions finely and allow to brown in three tablespoons of ghee in a large vessel. When brown add the bay leaves and cardamom and the chicken, lower the flame and cook gently for 10 minutes and remove from the fire.

3. In a clean vessel place one tablespoon of ghee, the ground masala, tomato pulp, turmeric and chilli powders. Roast over a low flame for 10 minutes till the masalas

are cooked. Add the saffron water and the whipped yoghurt. Then pour the gravy over the half cooked chicken and allow to simmer over a low fire for 25 minutes till tender. Add one cup water. Let the gravy thicken. Serve in a flat dish and sprinkle the peas over the chicken.

KHUSHBUDAR MARGHI

(Fragrant Poppy and Cashew Chicken)

Preparation Time: 25 mins.
Cooking Time: 35-40 mins. • Serves 6

1	kg. chicken. (legs and breast pieces, only)
4	silver leaves or vark
1	gm saffron
200	gms. cream or malai
3	green cardamoms crushed
4	bay leaves
3	whole star anise
10	whole black peppercorns
$\frac{1}{2}$"	piece cinnamon broken into two
$\frac{1}{2}$	teaspoon rosemary

100 gms. broken cashewnuts ⎫
1   tablespoon fennel seeds   ⎪
1   tablespoon poppy seeds   ⎪
1   tablespoon coriander seeds ⎬ grind finely
1   tablespoon chopped ginger ⎪
1   tablespoon javantri or mace ⎭
1   coconut milk removed
     salt
     ghee

1. Cut the chicken into decent sized pieces, marinate with salt and set aside.
2. Grind the spices finely with a little water.
3. Take a heavy bottomed vessel and place three tablespoons ghee in it. When hot add bay leaves, cardamoms, cinnamon, black peppercorns and rosemary powder. Lower flame and stir for two minutes. Add the finely ground masala and stir for seven minutes till cooked. Add the chicken pieces and mix vigorously for six minutes. Add all the coconut milk in a dribble to the pan. Heat the saffron on a griddle and crumble it onto the chicken and allow to simmer for 20 minutes.
4. Beat the cream and add it slowly to the cooked chicken till it is one with the gravy. Serve in a flat dish and cover with silver leaf.

PARSI PORA (Omelette)

Omelettes are made by people all over the world, in every country, and in practically every home. All women have their own little tricks and ways with them. In our family, omelettes are strictly had at breakfast time on days when the whole family is together and there is time to laugh and talk and take it easy. Sometimes, we eat omelettes for dinner when there is no interest in cooking a heavy meal. The Parsis in India make their basic, simple omelettes taste a little different by using a lot of fresh herbs. Freny adores prawn stuffed omelettes and I used to send tomato and mushroom stuffed omelettes as well as chicken stuffed omelettes to my clients. Cheese omelettes are very simple to make with a few green deseeded chillies thrown in for taste. Anyway try some of these omelettes out when you are too tired to cook or you have better things to do than slave over your stove.

Parsis normally carry rotli and poras on picnics and on train journeys and they even eat them on days when they are not supposed to eat mutton and chicken. So heres to omelettes!!!

PARSI PORO

(Parsi Omelettes)

Preparation Time: 8 mins.
Cooking Time: 20 mins. • Serves 4

6	eggs
2	small onions finely chopped or a packet of chives
3	tablespoons fresh coriander, finely chopped
1	tablespoon mint, finely chopped
3	green chillies, deseeded and finely chopped
$1/2$	teaspoon ginger-garlic paste
$1/2$	teaspoon turmeric powder
$1/2$	teaspoon pepper powder
1	teaspoon chilli powder
1	green mango finely chopped when in season
	salt to taste
	ghee

1. Take a round bowl and crack six large eggs into it. Add all the ingredients including salt to taste and mix well.

2. Take an iron tava or skillet and put a quarter cup of oil in it. Allow it to heat well, stir the mixture and pour one-fourth of it on the skillet. Allow the underside to become golden brown and then flip it over and cook it over medium heat. If the heat is too intense when you pour the egg mixture the omelette will burn and turn out raw.

3. Make four omelettes out of this mixture and serve them with chips, sour lime and buttered toast.

LEELI KERI NE VENGNANI AKOORI

(Akoori with Raw Mangoes and Brinjal)

Preparation Time: 20 mins.
Cooking Time: 30 mins. • Serves 6

8	eggs
1	brinjal long black skinned (250 gms.)
2	raw mangoes skinned and very finely chopped
3	large onions, finely chopped
4	green chillies, deseeded and chopped
$1/2$	bunch fresh coriander, finely chopped
1	bunch green garlic, finely chopped
$1/2$	teaspoon turmeric powder
$1/2$	teaspoon chilli powder
	ghee as needed
	salt to taste

1. Peel the brinjal, cut into four long strips and then finely slice the strips, wafer thin. Place in salted water.

2. Cut the onions and cook in two to three tablespoons ghee till soft and pink. Drain the brinjals in a sieve and wipe with a soft cloth. Then add them to the onions along with the mangoes, chillies, coriander, green garlic and spices. Cook covered on a low flame, stirring from time to time, till soft.

3. Whip the eggs, salt carefully as the brinjals have been soaked in salted water. Add the eggs to the thick vegetable mixture and scramble till soft and porridge like. Remove from the fire and serve immediately with hot rotlis.

AKOORI

Preparation Time: 8 mins.
Cooking Time: 15-20 mins. • Serves 4

6	eggs
2	medium sized onions
1	medium sized potato
1	large tomato
4	green chillies, deseeded
2	tablespoons chopped coriander
2	tablespoons cream or milk
3	dessertspoons ghee
	salt to taste

1. Chop the onion and potato very finely and fry in ghee till soft. Remove excess ghee.

2. Add finely chopped tomato, green chillies and coriander and allow to cook over a slow fire till the mixture becomes soft.

3. Beat the eggs, cream and salt and pour a steady trickle into the vegetables on the fire, stirring all the while. Remove as soon as the mixture begins to thicken. Do not allow to congeal. It should be soft.

4. Serve immediately with hot rotlis.

SOOKA BOOMLA NI AKOORI

(Akoori with Dried Bombay Ducks)

Preparation Time: 20 mins.
Cooking Time: 20 mins. • Serves 6

2	large dried Bombay ducks
8	eggs
2	large onions, sliced and deep fried
4	green chillies deseeded, and finely cut
$\frac{1}{2}$	bunch fresh coriander, finely chopped
$\frac{1}{2}$	teaspoon ginger-garlic paste
$\frac{1}{4}$	teaspoon turmeric powder
$\frac{1}{2}$	teaspoon chilli powder
2	tablespoons ghee
	salt to taste
	oil for frying

1. Soak the Bombay ducks in water for an hour after cleaning them and removing the centre bone. Shred into tiny pieces, wash twice and drain. Dry with a soft clean cloth. Deep fry in hot oil and place on absorbent paper.

2. Place two tablespoons ghee in a kadhai and add the chillies, coriander, garlic-ginger paste and spices and cook for two minutes. Add the fried onions and stir for two more minutes over a low flame.

3. Whip the eggs well, add salt to taste and pour it into the onion mixture. Stir vigorously for two to three minutes. When you feel that the egg mixture is slowly thickening add the fried Bombay ducks. Turn off the heat. Mix and serve with rice rotlis.

BOTI NI AKOORI

(Akoori with finely cut Mutton)

Preparation Time: 30 mins.
Cooking Time: 15 mins. • Serves 6

8	large eggs
150	gms. mutton, very finely cut and boiled soft
2	large onions, sliced and deep fried
4	green chillies, finely chopped
2	tablespoons green coriander
1	tablespoon mint, freshly cut
$1/_2$	teaspoon turmeric powder
$1/_2$	teaspoon black pepper powder
$1/_2$	teaspoon dhansakh masala
3	tablespoons butter
	salt to taste

1. Place a heavy kadhai on the stove and put in the green chillies, mint, coriander, spices and butter. Heat over a low flame. Cook for three minutes, add the tiny boiled mutton pieces, fried onions and allow to cook for five minutes. The mutton should not stick to the pan. Keep turning it till it is nice and red.

2. Beat the eggs in a bowl. Add salt to taste and two tablespoons of water or milk. Pour in a steady stream over the meat masala with one hand, whilst vigorously stirring the contents with the right hand. Remove from the pan whilst the mixture is soft and spongy.

PANEER CHARVELA EDA SATHE

(Scrambled Eggs with Paneer)

Preparation Time: 10 mins.
Cooking Time: 15-18 mins. • Serves 4-6

200	gms. paneer or cottage cheese chopped finely or grated
6	eggs
1	onion, finely chopped
2	tablespoons coriander, finely chopped
4	finely chopped green chillies, deseeded
$1/_2$	teaspoon chilli powder
$1/_2$	teaspoon black pepper powder
$1/_2$	teaspoon ginger-garlic paste
2	teaspoons butter or ghee
	salt to taste

Our family is fond of cottage cheese and use it in a variety of ways. This recipe with eggs is eaten with toast at breakfast.

1. Place the butter or ghee in a frying pan and cook the onion till it is soft and pink. Toss in the ginger-garlic paste and mix well. Then put in the chopped chillies, coriander, pepper and chilli powders and lastly the paneer. Remove from the stove after 3 minutes.

2. Beat the eggs with a little salt. Whisk well and replace the frying pan over a low flame.

3. Allow the egg to trickle into the pan and stir the mixture non-stop. Allow to form into a soft-spongy mixture and remove from the flame.

4. Serve immediately. The mixture should be soft – if you cook it too dry there will be no pleasure in eating it.

TARKARI-PER-EDA

(Eggs on Mixed Vegetables)

Preparation Time: 30 mins.
Cooking Time: 40 mins. • Serves 6-8.

12	eggs
1	cup carrots, boiled and diced
1	cup french beans, boiled and diced
1/2	cup potatoes, boiled and diced
1/2	cup tomatoes, chopped
1	tablespoon coriander, chopped
1	tablespoon ginger, chopped
1	tablespoon carraway seeds
2	large onions
1/2	teaspoon turmeric powder
1	teaspoon chilli powder
1	tablespoon sugarcane vinegar
	salt
	pepper
	ghee

1. Dice the onion and fry in four tablespoons of ghee till golden. Add carraway seeds, coriander, tomatoes, turmeric, ginger and chilli powder and fry for a further five minutes after which toss in all the boiled vegetables, mash them and sprinkle with salt. Cover and cook for about 10 minutes. When the ghee has all been absorbed lower the flame and add the vinegar and stir.

2. Take a flat thali or pan and spread the vegetables in a thick layer.

3. Whip the eggs with a whisk. Add a pinch of salt and pepper and spread evenly over the vegetables. Cover and allow to cook on a slow heat for 7-10 minutes. Cut into twelve squares or more and serve while hot.

GHEE TOORIA PER EDA

(Eggs on Smooth Skinned Gourd)

Preparation Time: 15 mins.
Cooking Time: 25-30 mins. • Serves 4-6

6	eggs
700	gms. or 3 large gourds
300	gms. or 4 tomatoes
200	gms. onions, finely chopped
100	gms. or a small bunch fresh coriander, finely chopped
1	teaspoon ginger-garlic paste
1	teaspoon green chillies, finely cut
1/2	teaspoon cumin crushed
3	tablespoons oil

1. Skin and finely chop the gourds and tomatoes. Wash and chop the coriander.

2. Place the oil in a flat bottomed pan and add curry leaves if desired. Add the onions and cook over a medium flame till soft. Add the ginger-garlic paste and cook for a further five minutes. Add the cumin seeds and stir for two minutes. Add the chopped tomatoes, gourds and a pinch of salt to taste. Cover and cook over a very slow flame till soft.

3. Before you sit to eat, spread the vegetable in a fry pan and make six holes. Heat the vegetable, crack an egg in each hole, sprinkle salt, cover and cook till eggs are done.

SALI PER EDA

(Chicken in a Haystack)

Preparation Time: 10 mins.
Cooking Time: 15 mins. • Serves 6-8

200 gms. potato shoestrings or sali.
4   large red tomatoes
2   large onions, chopped finely
$1/_2$ cup coriander, chopped
1   tablespoon mint, freshly chopped
1   tablespoon green chillies, finely chopped
2   capsicums sliced
1   teaspoon red chilli powder
1   teaspoon sugar
1   tablespoon tomato ketchup
3   tablespoons ghee or butter
6-8 eggs
      salt to taste

Note: You can buy readymade shoestrings/Sali or make them yourself. I make my own and store them in an airtight jar. They can remain for almost two months.

1. Cook the finely chopped onions in the ghee or butter till soft. Add the finely chopped tomatoes, capsicums, chillies, coriander, chilli powder, sugar, ketchup and salt and cook till soft. Add half a teacup of water.

2. Take a large skillet and spread out the mixture. Make as many holes in the mixture as you have eggs. Place the mixture over a low flame.

3. Crack each egg separately and lower it carefully onto the mixture so that the yolk is placed in the hole. Do this with all the eggs, sprinkle with the mint and a little water and cover the skillet and cook till firm over low heat. Grate black pepper over the eggs, serve on the top of the shoestrings.

BAFELA EDA NI CURRY

(Boiled Egg Curry)

Preparation Time: 25 mins.
Cooking Time: 20 mins. • Serves 6

10   boiled eggs
$1/_2$ coconut, milk removed
4   potatoes
2   large onions, finely ground
2   large tomatoes, chopped
$1/_2$ coconut, grated
10   Kashmiri chillies
4   tablespoons coriander seeds
1   tablespoon white sesame seeds
1   teaspoon poppy seeds
$1/_2$ teaspoon turmeric powder
$1/_4$ cup skinned monkey nuts
$1/_4$ cup skinned gram or chana
      jaggery (size of a sour lime)
10   cloves garlic
2   sprigs curry patta
3   tablespoons oil

grind together with half-cup water

1. Heat the oil in a dekchi along with the curry leaves, add finely chopped tomatoes. When the oil starts sizzling put in the finely ground masala and onions also, and allow to roast till red. Add salt. Stir well so that the masala does not burn and stick to the bottom of the vessel.

2. Chop the potatoes into cubes and add them to the masala along with the coconut milk and two cups of water. Stir and allow to cook over a medium flame. Cook till potatoes are tender. Add more water as required.

3. Shell the eggs and sprinkle them with a pinch of saffron colour. Heat one tablespoon of oil in a frying pan and roll the eggs in the oil for a moment and then place them in the cooked curry.

KERA PER EDA

(Eggs on Fried Bananas)

Preparation Time: 5 mins.
Cooking Time: 15 mins. • Serves 4-6

1/2	teaspoon cardamom-nutmeg powder
6	ripe cooking bananas
2	tablespoons fried raisins
2	tablespoons rose water
2	tablespoons sugar
6	eggs
	ghee

1. Take very ripe cooking bananas. Roll them on a wooden board, peel and slice them.

2. Take a heavy fry pan, place half a cup ghee in it and when hot fry the banana slices till soft and golden. Remove from ghee and mash the cooked bananas till soft. Mix in the sugar, spice powder, raisins and rose water. Spread the mixture in a heavy fry pan.

3. Make six shallow holes in the banana mixture and heat on a low flame. Sprinkle one tablespoon of water. When the mixture becomes warm crack one egg at a time in a saucer and lower it into the hole in the mixture. After all the eggs have been used up, sprinkle a little salt, cover and cook till the eggs are solid.

4. Serve immediately with hot toast or rotlis.

BHIDA-PER-EDA

(Eggs on Lady fingers)

Preparation Time: 5-7 mins.
Cooking Time: 7-10 mins. • Serves 4-6

6	eggs
350 gms.	small tender lady fingers
1	medium sized onion
1/2	cup tomatoes chopped
1	tablespoon vinegar
1/2	teaspoon pepper powder
1	tablespoon sugar
2	dessertspoons coriander, finely chopped
	salt
	refined oil

1. Wash, salt and finely slice the lady fingers and deep fry them. Drain and keep aside.

2. Cut the onion into half and slice finely. Deep fry in the same ghee. Drain and keep aside.

3. Take a large frying pan and spread the onions and the lady fingers. Place on a low flame. Sprinkle pepper powder, chopped tomatoes and sugar dissolved in vinegar over the lady fingers. Make six holes in the spread vegetables and gently break the eggs into the depressions. Sprinkle salt and fresh coriander over them and put on a low flame.

4. Sprinkle two dessertspoons of water, cover and cook for about 5-7 minutes, or place in a hot oven for 7-10 minutes.

Sali Ne Jerdaloo-Ma-Gos (8
Tamotar-Ma-Bhejoo (71
Rotli (1
Gajar-Mewa-Nu-Achaar (
Papeto Kaleji (72
Lagan-sara-Istew (102

EDA CHUTNEY NA PATTICE

(Egg and Chutney Pattice)

Preparation Time: 25 mins.
Cooking Time: 40 mins. • Serves 5-6

For the Covering
500 gms. mashed potatoes
2 tablespoons fresh coriander, finely chopped
$1/2$ teaspoon black pepper powder
salt to taste

For the Filling
8 hard boiled eggs each cut into two
1 portion green chutney (see page 130)
5 eggs
2 cups breadcrumbs
oil for deep frying

1. Mix the mashed potatoes with the coriander, pepper powder and salt to taste. Divide into sixteen equal balls.

2. Take each ball and place it in the palm of your left hand and flatten it out into a circle. Place a heaped tablespoon of green chutney in the centre and half a boiled egg on top of the chutney. Carefully fold the potato covering into an oval shape.

3. Beat the raw eggs. Place a kadhai half full of oil on the stove. Roll the pattice in the breadcrumbs and dip in the beaten egg and fry in the hot oil, till golden in colour.

KOLMI BHARELO PORO

(Prawn Stuffed Omelettes)

Preparation Time: 8 mins.
Cooking Time: 30 mins. • Serves 4-6

8	eggs	for the omelettes
$1/4$	teaspoon pepper	
	salt	
	ghee	
1	stalk celery, finely chopped	for the stuffing
1	cup prawns, deveined, washed	
2	large tomatoes skinned and deseeded	
2	green chillies, deseeded and finely chopped	
4	spring onions or a packet of chives	
$1/2$	teaspoon chilli powder	
	salt	

1. Chop the spring onions, celery and skinned tomatoes finely and cook in two tablespoons of ghee till soft.

2. Add the prawns, chilli powder, deseeded green chillies and salt to taste and cook till the mixture is thick and prawns soft.

3. Beat the eggs, two at a time with a pinch of pepper powder and salt in your mixie and pour into a non-stick pan in which you have heated one tablespoon ghee. Shake the pan and allow the omelette to cook over a slow fire till settled.

4. Divide the prawn mixture into four portions. Place one-fourth of it on one half of the omelette as it is cooking. When the bottom side is fairly firm place a spatula below the omelette which has no filling and invert it over the stuffed half. Cook for a couple of minutes more, overturn and then slide it onto a plate and serve immediately. Make the three other omelettes in the same manner.

Goonamai-No-Keri-No-Pulao (90)

OF BRAINS, LIVERS AND MUTTON

One of the best brain dishes I ever ate was in a huge restaurant in Antwerp, Belgium. The brain had been cut into square pieces and steamed and served around salad greens and watercress. It made a light and appetising dish.

The few recipes that I have included in this book are my children's favourites. Kurush, my eldest son loves to eat hot brain cutlets, whereas my daughter Freny and son Daraius prefer brain cooked in coriander and tomatoes.

Liver is a tougher nut to crack. You must never overcook it. It should only be on the fire for five to seven minutes. If cooking liver in a potato gravy, cook till potatoes are soft, then braise the liver separately and add it to the cooked gravy. Liver roasted over a coal fire can be delicious, but it must be eaten there and then. You can't cook liver and eat it later on. The taste is totally lost. Actually, the best way to deal with liver is to marinate the pieces in salt and ginger-garlic paste and cook it in a little ghee for five minutes only.

The brain you cook must be as fresh as possible and you must clean, wash and marinate them immediately they arrive in your kitchen. Refrigerate till you are ready to cook them. The red membrane which covers the brain must be completely removed. The little triangular piece above the brain must always be checked for worms.

It is dangerous to order brain dishes in a restaurant. It is best avoided.

BHEJA-NA-CUTLES

(Brain Cutlets)

Preparation Time: 20 mins.
Cooking Time: 20 mins. • Serves 6

6	sheeps' brains
1	tablespoon coriander, chopped
2	teaspoons ginger and garlic paste
1	teaspoon turmeric powder
2	teaspoons chilli powder
3	eggs
$1/2$	cup bread crumbs
	ghee or vanaspati
	salt to taste

1. Wash brains and then skin carefully. Wash again and cut each vertically into two pieces. Apply salt, ginger-garlic paste, turmeric and chilli powder. Set aside.

2. Take a shallow vessel, put in half a cup of water and the coriander and arrange the brain carefully so that the pieces do not break up. Cover the vessel and bring to a quick boil or keep the vessel on a low fire till all the water has been absorbed. Remove and cool.

3. Spread the bread crumbs on a wooden board. Put a piece of brain on the board, flatten it with the palm of your hand or a spatula or broad kitchen knife. Turn over to coat the other side with bread crumbs and keep aside. When all the pieces have been similarly treated, put 2 cups ghee in a deep vessel and heat.

4. Break the eggs in a bowl. Add a pinch of salt, pepper and coriander and beat stiffly. When the ghee begins to smoke, dip the brain pieces into the beaten egg and fry till golden brown.

TAMOTA-MA-BHEJOO

(Brains cooked with Tomatoes)

Preparation Time: 20 mins.
Cooking Time: 25 mins. • Serves 6

6   sheeps' brains
2   teaspoons ginger-garlic paste
500 gms. large ripe tomatoes, skinned and
     deseeded
6   medium sized onions
8   green chillies
1   large bunch coriander
1   teaspoon turmeric powder
1$\frac{1}{2}$ teaspoon chilli powder
$\frac{1}{2}$ teaspoon black pepper, freshly ground
     salt to taste
3   tablespoons ghee

1. Wash the brains, skin and remove all the red membrane and after washing again, cut each into four pieces. Apply salt, ginger-garlic paste and keep aside.

2. Peel the onions and cut into halves and slice thinly. Put into a pan or heavy vessel and deep fry in the ghee till brown. Drain and set aside.

3. Chop chillies and coriander finely. Halve tomatoes, deseed and cut into small pieces.

4. Place the fried onions in a heavy skillet. Add pepper, turmeric, chilli powder and green chillies and stir. Next add the tomatoes. Stir and cook for five minutes till soft. Add the chopped coriander and brain. Mix lightly, cover and cook for 10-15 minutes until no gravy remains. Shake the pan from side to side so that the brain is evenly cooked. Taste for salt.

5. Remove carefully onto a serving dish and eat immediately.

LASAN-NE-KOTHMIR-NU-BHEJOO

(Brains with fresh Garlic and Coriander)

Preparation Time: 20 mins.
Cooking Time: 15-20 mins. • Serves 6

6   sheeps' brains
4   onions
1   teaspoon turmeric powder
3   cups green coriander, freshly chopped
1   teaspoon ginger-garlic paste
1   pod garlic — finely sliced or 3 bunches fresh garlic
1   tablespoon cuminseeds ⎱ grind together with
6   green chillies   ⎰ 2 tablespoons
8   black peppercorns   water
     salt
     oil

1. Wash the brains and remove all the skin and red portion in the brain. Wash well, apply salt and cut each brain into five pieces. Marinate in the ginger-garlic paste and set aside.

2. Cut each onion into two pieces and slice finely. Deep fry along with the sliced garlic (if using dried garlic) till golden brown and set aside.

3. Take three tablespoons of oil in which the onions were fried and place the oil in a large fry pan. Fry the ground masala and turmeric in it and if necessary add half a cup of water. When the masala is cooked add a pinch of salt, coriander, fresh garlic if using it and the fried onions. Make an even level of the pans contents, turn the flame low and drop the pieces of brain on top. Shake the pan from side to side and cover till the brains are cooked. Taste for salt.

4. Remove with the help of a spatula onto a serving dish and eat immediately.

BHUNJELI KALEJI

(Skewered Roasted Goats Liver)

Preparation Time: 15 mins.
Cooking Time: 15-20 mins. • Serves 4

1	large goats liver	
6	Kashmiri chillies	
1	tablespoon chopped fresh ginger	
1	tablespoon chopped garlic	grind in
1	tablespoon cumin seed	$1/4$ cup
$1/2$	tablespoon coriander seeds	vinegar
$1/2$	tablespoon sesame seeds	
1	green cardamom	
$1/6$	nutmeg	
	salt	
	oil	

1. Skin the liver and discard the white ligaments. Wash and cut into rectangular 1" pieces.

2. Grind the spices in a little vinegar till soft. Apply salt on the liver and marinate for 1 hour in the masala.

3. Place 6-8 pieces on each metal skewer and prepare the pieces for roasting. Heat a chula half filled with red hot coals and place the skewers across the chula. Keep turning several times till the liver is red and tender to eat. Please control the coals. If they are hot and black your liver will burn up.

PAPETO-KALEJI

(Masala Potato Liver)

Preparation Time: 10 mins.
Cooking Time: 20-30 mins. • Serves 6-8

2	large goat livers
500 gms.	potatoes
300 gms.	tomatoes
15	cloves garlic
10	red Kashmiri chillies, deseeded
2	teaspoons turmeric powder
$2^1/2$	teaspoons Parsi dhansakh powder
$1/2$"	cinnamon
$1/4$	cup vinegar
1	tablespoon ginger-garlic paste
	ghee
	salt to taste

1. Soak the red chillies in the vinegar.

2. Peel the potatoes, cut into small square pieces, wash, salt and deep fry till golden. Drain and keep aside.

3. Wash livers and after removing the skin cut into square pieces. Marinate in salt ginger-garlic paste.

4. Grind together the red chillies, garlic, turmeric, cinnamon and Parsi dhansakh powders in the vinegar. Do not use water.

5. Take a clean vessel and add to it three tablespoons of ghee in which the potatoes had been fried. When hot fry the ground masala till an aroma emanates from it and then add the liver and stir for three minutes. Lower the flame. Cover and cook for five minutes.

6. Skin the tomatoes and cut into small pieces and add to the liver. When the liver is cooked add the fried potatoes. Stir and serve.

KHAROO GOS

(Basic Mutton Gravy)

Preparation Time: 10 mins.
Cooking Time: 25 mins. • Serves 8-10

1	kg. mutton pieces with leg bones
1	tablespoon ginger-garlic paste
2-3	large onions
1"	stick cinnamon
10	peppercorns
3	bay leaves
5	whole dried red chillies, preferably Kashmiri chillies. Do not remove the stalks
3	cloves
$\frac{1}{2}$	teaspoon mace or javantri powder
	salt
	oil

1. Wash the meat and marinate in ginger-garlic paste with salt for half an hour.

2. Cut the onions finely, and roast to a light golden colour in $\frac{1}{2}$ cup oil. Add the whole masala and fry well with the onions for a few minutes. Toss in the meat and cook till it acquires a reddish tinge.

3. Place in a pressure cooker along with 3-4 cups of water and allow to cook till soft.

This mutton gravy is served topped with various vegetables.

   (i)   Serve with fried lady fingers.

   (ii) Serve with fried potato chips.

   (iii) Serve with boiled green peas.

   (iv) Serve with fried sooran or yam.

   (v)   Best of all serve in the following manner:

Take 500 gms. sweet potatoes. Boil, skin and cut into round, thick slices. Deep fry and set aside.

Make a thick syrup with 1 cup sugar, 2 cups water and 4 cardamoms coarsely crushed. When the syrup boils and begins to thicken put in the fried sweet potatoes and remove the pan from the fire.

Spread the mutton, gravy on a flat dish and top with the sweet potatoes.

This is a delicious and unusual dish to try out on your family.

BAPAIJI NO GOS-NO-RAS

(Grandma's Mutton Ras or Gravy)

Preparation Time: 30 mins.
Cooking Time: 45 mins. • Serves 4-6

500	gms. mutton chunks
200	gms. potato pieces
100	gms. sliced carrots
50	gms. green peas
1	small stick celery cut into 3" pieces
1	tablespoon ginger-garlic paste
1	coconut milk removed
1	tablespoon chilli powder
1	tablespoon garam masala
4	large tomatoes made into pulp
3	large onions, finely chopped
	oil
	salt to taste

1. Clean and wash the meat. Apply salt, ginger-garlic paste and set aside.

2. Chop the onions finely and place in a pressure cooker with half cup oil. When the onion turns golden add the mutton chunks and stir the onions well. Lower the flame and add the cut potatoes, celery, sliced carrots, washed green peas, milk of one coconut, the spice powders, tomato pulp and two cups water. Taste for salt and close the pressure cooker and cook till the meat is tender.

MAMMA NO BAFAAT

(Mothers Mutton Bafaat)

Preparation Time: 40 mins.
Cooking Time: 40 mins. • Serves 10-12

1	kg. mutton chunks
1	tablespoon ginger-garlic paste
1	kg. tiny potatoes
3	medium sized onions
10	large cloves of garlic
15	red Kashmiri chillies
6	cloves
1	teaspoon turmeric powder
1"	piece cinnamon
4	cardamoms
20	peppercorns
$\frac{1}{2}$	kopra ground
$\frac{1}{2}$	a nutmeg
$\frac{1}{2}$	cup almonds or cashew nuts
4	boiled eggs
4	sliced capsicums
2	tablespoons sugar
2	carrots, sliced and boiled
$1\frac{1}{2}$	cups curd
	ghee
	salt to taste

} grind together in a little water

1. Clean the meat and cut into $1\frac{1}{2}$" cubes. Wash, apply salt; ginger-garlic paste, and keep aside.

2. Peel the potatoes and keep whole in salted water. Deep fry till golden brown. Drain and keep aside. Slice and fry the capsicums.

3. Grind together finely, the kopra, turmeric, garlic, chillies, cardamoms, cloves, cinnamon, peppercorns, nutmeg and cashews in a little water. When the paste is fine and soft apply it to the meat and keep in a cool place for 1-2 hours. Mix the sugar in the curd and allow to dissolve.

4. Chop the onion and fry till brown. Add the meat and ground masala and fry till all the ghee is absorbed and the meat is red-brown. Add 4 cups of water and cook in a pressure cooker till soft.

5. When the meat is cooked and a little gravy remains, whip and add the curd and the fried potatoes. Mix well and serve as soon as possible. The curd may not be used if you do not like it.

6. Top the dish with the hard boiled eggs and slices of fried capsicums and the boiled carrot slices.

SOONAMAI-NI-PAPETI-KANDI-MA GOS

(Soonamai's Baby Onions and Baby Potatoes in Mutton Gravy)

Preparation Time: 20 mins.
Cooking Time: 30-40 mins. • Serves 8-10

250 gms. onions
250 gms. papeti (tiny potatoes)
250 gms. kandi (tiny onions)
1   kg. mutton cubes
300 gms. tomatoes, chopped
1   teaspoon pepper powder
2   cloves whole
2   green cardamoms whole
1   tablespoon ginger-garlic paste
2   tablespoons coriander, chopped
    oil
    salt

1. Boil the tiny potatoes; skin the tiny onions; chop the large onions finely.

2. Deep fry the tiny potatoes and onions separately in a kadhai. Drain. Take some of the leftover oil, about half cup and place in a dekchi and fry the finely chopped onions until soft and pink.

3. Wash the mutton and marinate in salt and ginger-garlic paste. Then add to the cooked onion along with the pepper powder, cloves and cardamom. Fry well. Add water and tomatoes and cook in a pressure cooker till mutton is soft. Add the fried baby onions and potatoes and simmer on the stove for ten minutes till the mixture thickens. Top with chopped coriander.

GOS MALAI-DAR

(Mutton Cooked with Cream)

Preparation Time: 15 mins.
Cooking Time: 35-40 mins. • Serves 8-10

2   gms. saffron
1   kg. chunks of leg with nali
1   tablespoon ginger-garlic paste
200 gms. thick cream
100 gms. broken cashewnuts ⎫
1   teaspoon cumin seeds, roasted ⎪
1   teaspoon fennel seeds, roasted ⎪
1   teaspoon poppy seeds, roasted ⎪ grind
10 black pepper corns ⎬ together
2   green cardamoms ⎪
6   green chillies deseeded ⎪
$1/_2$ cup finely chopped ⎪
    coriander leaves ⎭
2   large onions
4   bay leaves
$2 1/_2$" pieces of cinnamon
    salt
    ghee

1. Chop the onions and place in a vessel with half a cup of ghee and cook till soft and pink. Wash the mutton, apply ginger-garlic paste, salt and add it to the onions and fry till the mutton is red. Either cook mutton over a stove for two hours or cook in a pressure cooker in four cups of water.

2. After the mutton has cooked to a soft consistency, heat a quarter cup of ghee in a pan and fry the masala. Add the bay leaves, cinnamon and cook over a low fire. Add the cooked mutton and two cups soup. Put on simmer for twenty minutes. Heat the saffron on a tava and crumble into the gravy. When the gravy becomes nice and thick remove from the fire. Just before serving, reheat the gravy and mix in the lightly whisked cream and cook for two more minutes. Serve at once.

BHUNJELI-GOS-NI-TANG

(Roast Leg of Lamb)

Preparation Time: 1 hr.
Cooking Time: 2¹/₂-3 hrs. • Serves 10

3	kg. leg of lamb with the cysts removed
20	garlic cloves
2	tablespoons ginger-garlic paste
4	bay leaves
6	whole Kashmiri chillies
3	green cardamoms, coarsely crushed
15	black peppercorns, coarsely ground
2"	piece of cinnamon
4	cloves
	salt
	ghee

1. Wash the leg. Trim the skin and with a fork poke the flesh all over. Rub salt and ginger-garlic paste over the leg and keep for one hour.

2. Take a sharp knife make tiny slits in the flesh and insert a garlic clove into the slits.

3. Crush the black pepper, cloves, cardamoms, coarsely and apply over the leg. Fry the leg in 1¹/₂ cups ghee along with the bay leaves and whole Kashmiri chillies till red.

4. Place in an oven at 375°F for 3-4 hours. Keep turning the leg and basting it with the ghee for the first half an hour. Then add one cup water at a time and turn the leg till it is tender. Insert a sharp knife into the leg to see if its done. Indian mutton is tough, so in case it doesn't cook as you would wish it, place in a pressure cooker after the first hour.

5. Scrape the pan in which the leg was roasted. Add two cups water, a little salt, and two tablespoons cornflour. Mix well and heat. Stir while the sauce is cooking. Taste for salt. Serve with green vegetables.

MASOOR-MA-GOS

(Lentils cooked with Mutton)

Preparation Time: 10 mins.
Cooking Time: 35 mins. • Serves 6-8

300	gms. black lentils or masoor
300	gms. mutton (chunks)
4	large tomatoes, finely chopped
2	large onions, finely chopped
4	green chillies, finely cut
¹/₂	cup coriander, chopped
1	sprig curry leaves
2	teaspoons ginger-garlic paste
1¹/₂	teaspoons turmeric powder
2¹/₂	teaspoons chilli powder
2	teaspoons Parsi dhansakh masala
2	teaspoons sambar masala
¹/₄	cup tamarind juice
¹/₄	cup jaggery
	salt to taste
	refined oil or ghee

1. Wash the mutton thoroughly and marinate in salt and ginger-garlic paste. Wash the masoor. Place both into a pressure cooker with 6 cups of water along with the green chillies, turmeric and chilli powders. Cook till the mutton is soft and tender.

2. Place onions in a dekchi with half cup oil. Add curry leaves and cook onions till brown. Add the tomatoes, Parsi masala and sambar and lower heat. Add ¹/₂ cup water and simmer for 5 minutes.

3. Add the mutton and masoor from the cooker. Stir, do not mash the mutton pieces. Once the mixture starts bubbling add the tamarind juice and jaggery. Allow the masoor to boil for a further 2 minutes before serving. Garnish with coriander leaves.

4. Serve with pure ghee, pickles and rotlis.

SARO MUTTON BAFAAT

(Richman's Mutton Bafaat)

Preparation Time: 35 mins.
Cooking Time: 2½ hrs. • Serves 10-12

This is a Parsi speciality and I have never eaten meat which tasted just so anywhere else in India.

750 gms. onions finely chopped
1½ kg. mutton leg cut into 1½" pieces
1½ tablespoons ginger-garlic paste
1 kg. potatoes, peeled and washed
½ kernel of dried coconut
8 Kashmiri chillies
4 green chillies
15 black peppercorns ⎱ finely grind
2" piece cinnamon ⎰ with ¼ cup
1 teaspoon carraway seeds   vinegar
7 cloves
1 teaspoon turmeric powder
½ kg. tomatoes, skinned, deseeded and finely chopped
1 bunch coriander, finely chopped
¼ cup vinegar
¼ cup sugar
1 cup sesame or peanut oil
curry leaves
salt

1. Take a heavy bottomed pan or dekchi. Pour in the oil, add the chopped onions and fry till golden brown.

2. Marinate the mutton in salt and ginger-garlic paste.

3. Grind all the spices and dried coconut in ¼ cup vinegar. If necessary add water.

4. When the onion is soft, add meat and allow to cook on a slow fire for 1 hour till the meat is tender adding water every little while as required.

5. Fry the meat in a pressure cooker along with the ground masala. Add tomatoes, coriander, potatoes, cut each into 6 pieces, and the curry leaves. Add sufficient water and pressure cook for 15

minutes on a slow fire. Open the cooker, add sugar, vinegar and stir and serve.

KHARA-GOS MA KAMODIO-KAND

(Mutton Gravy with Fried Purple Yam)

Preparation Time: 10 mins.
Cooking Time: 35 mins. • Serves 6

500 gms. leg mutton chunks
350 gms. purple yam
200 gms. tomato pulp
2 large onions, finely chopped
1 tablespoon ginger-garlic paste
3 bay leaves
5 black peppercorns ⎱ roasted and dry
1" piece cinnamon ⎰ ground in a
3 green cardamom seeds   mixer-grinder
¼ nutmeg
1 tablespoon white flour or maida
200 gms. ghee
salt

1. Skin the yam and cut into 1" square pieces. Soak in salted water, dry with a cloth towel and fry in ghee till soft.

2. Take three tablespoons of ghee after the yam has been fried and place the onions and bay leaves in a large pan. When the onions turn golden in colour add the salted meat covered with ginger-garlic paste. Lower flame and allow to simmer in its own juice for seven minutes. Add flour and fry for two minutes. Add tomatoes and three cups water, cook in a pressure cooker till soft and tender.

3. Place the mutton in a flat dish, sprinkle spices on top and cover with fried yam.

CHORA MA KHARIA

(Trotters with Black Eyed Beans)

Preparation Time: 30 mins.
Cooking Time: 1½ hrs. • Serves 6-8

12 front leg trotters each cut into 3 pieces
350 gms. black eyed peas or chowli beans
4 large onions, finely chopped
3 large tomatoes, chopped
1½ tablespoons ginger-garlic paste
½ grated coconut
7 kashmiri chillies ⎫
6 cloves ⎪ Grind
1" cinnamon piece ⎬ together
3 green cardamoms ⎪ in a quarter
10 black peppercorns ⎪ cup of
1 teaspoon mace powder ⎭ water
2 green chillies, deseeded, finely chopped
2 tablespoons fresh mint, finely chopped
  salt
  refined oil

1. Wash and clean the trotters and see no hair sticks to the skin. Wash three times and marinate in the ginger-garlic paste and salt for 15 minutes. Place in a pressure cooker with 6 cups of water and cook till very soft and tender.

2. Cook the onion in three-quarter cup oil, in a heavy bottomed vessel. When the onions are golden-brown add ground masala and fry over a low flame till red. Add the tomatoes and cook till soft.

3. Wash the beans twice and soak in water overnight to double its size. Place in a pressure cooker along with the coconut gravy and 5 cups of the soup from the cooked trotters. Add salt to taste and cook till beans are soft.

4. Empty the beans and trotters in a large, heavy bottomed vessel and cook very slowly for half an hour. Sprinkle green chillies and mint and serve with sour lime wedges.

MUTTON-NO-BAFAAT

(Savoury Mutton with Boiled Eggs)

Preparation Time: 30 mins.
Cooking Time: 35 mins. • Serves 8-10

1 kg. mutton chunks with nali
8 boiled eggs cut into halves
5 large potatoes chopped into cubes and fried
3 carrots cut into slices and fried
¼ dried coconut
8 Kashmiri chillies
1 large garlic pod ⎫ grind
2" fresh ginger ⎪ together
1 teaspoon black peppercorns ⎬ with a
4 green cardamoms ⎪ little sugar-
¼ nutmeg ⎪ cane
100 gms. broken cashew nuts ⎪ vinegar
125 gms. seedless raisins ⎭
2 large onions, finely chopped
4 large tomatoes, skinned and deseeded
3 bay leaves
1 teaspoon sugar
  salt
  oil

1. Wash the mutton, apply salt and set aside. Grind the masala finely.

2. Place the onion, bay leaves and half a cup oil in a heavy bottomed vessel. Cook till the onions turn pink and soft and then add the ground masala and fry it till red. Add the mutton and lower the flame. Mix well and allow to cook for ten minutes. When the mutton has been well coated with the masala, toss in the chopped tomatoes. Allow to cook on the same low flame for seven minutes. Then add two cups water, sugar, cover well and allow to cook till the mutton is tender. You will need to add fresh water as mutton takes two to two and a half hours to tenderise.

3 Place the mutton and its thick gravy on a flat dish and top with the boiled eggs and fried potatoes and carrots.

KISMIS-KHIMA-NA-PATTICE

(Raisin and Mince Pattice)

Preparation Time: 40 mins.
Cooking Time: 45 mins. • Serves 16-18

When we were children our grandmother Cooverbai Frenchman used to make this delicious dish for us, mainly on our birthdays. We had two dear next door neighbours Jeroo Soli and their mother Mrs. Dina Dastur who would invite us for dinner on their birthdays. She would call a Lalia cook Ramji to cook for them. He was very good at his job and I always went home and protested as to why we never put nuts and raisins in our khima pattice.

500 gms. raw or boiled mince meat.
1   kg. potatoes
200 gms. tomatoes, peeled and deseeded
2   tablespoons malt vinegar with 2 tablespoons sugar
$1/4$ tea cup tomato sauce
2   large onions
$1/4$ cup washed, chopped coriander
1   tablespoon fresh mint, finely chopped
1   teaspoon red Kashmiri chilli powder
$1/2$ teaspoon black pepper powder
1   teaspoon Parsi dhansakh powder
$1/2$ cup raisins, washed
$1/4$ cup charoli
1   tablespoon ginger-garlic paste
1-2 cups bread crumbs
4-6 eggs
2   teaspoons cornflour
    oil for frying
    salt to taste

1. Wash the potatoes and boil them in the pressure cooker till soft. When cooked, drain the water, peel and mash well till soft and fluffy. Mix in a little salt, black pepper and chopped coriander about $1/4$ teaspoon or so. Roll into a ball and set aside.

2. Chop the onions finely and place in a saucepan along with 3 tablespoons of oil. Cook on a medium flame till soft and golden. Add the powdered masalas.

3. Mix the mince with the ginger-garlic paste and salt to taste and fry well in the onion mixture. Add the chopped tomatoes and $1/2$ cup water at a time and cook till soft. When all the gravy has evaporated, add the tomato sauce, vinegar, sugar, dhansakh masala, fresh coriander, mint, chilli, black pepper powder, raisins and charoli. Mix well and cook till mince is tender.

4. Divide the mashed potato into equal sized balls. Size should depend upon your personal taste and requirements.

5. Grease both your hands with a little oil and take a potato ball and flatten it on the palm of your left hand. Place over a tablespoon of mince mixture onto it and fold the edges of the potato into a nice round ball. Then flatten it on a wooden board from both sides and cover with the bread crumbs and set aside. After you have finished up all your mince mixture, beat two eggs at a time with a pinch of cornflour in a soup plate.

6. Heat oil in a kadhai or a large fry pan. When the oil is hot dip the pattice into the beaten eggs and fry till golden brown.

7. Serve hot as a snack or at meal times with black masoor dal and spring onions and green sour limes.

KESRI KABAB
JERDALOO-NA-RAS-MA
(Meatballs in Apricot Gravy)

Preparation Time: 35 mins.
Cooking Time: 45-50 mins. • Serves 4-6

1	gm. saffron
250	gms. mince
100	gms. dried apricots soaked overnight in water
3	large onions
5	large tomatoes
$1/4$	cup garlic, chopped
$1/4$	cup fresh coriander, chopped
$1/4$	cup fresh mint
3	large Kashmiri chillies with stalks
1	teaspoon ginger-garlic paste
1	teaspoon black pepper powder
6	slices bread
4	eggs
3	oranges sliced;
1	lettuce
	ghee
	salt
	oil

1. Heat the saffron on a tava till crisp. Steep in 1 cup of hot water.

2. Mix the mince with the garlic-ginger paste, black pepper and salt to taste. Add one finely chopped onion and half the coriander and mint. Soak the bread slices for five minutes in water. Then crush the bread and pulp it and squeeze all the water out. Add saffron. Mix it in the mince alongwith the three beaten eggs. Taste for salt.

3. Wet your hands and make tiny meatballs. First try to fry one in hot oil. In case it disintegrates add an extra egg.

4. Fry the whole lot of meatballs in small batches, in hot oil and set aside.

5. Take a saucepan and pour half cup of oil in which the meatballs had been fried. Chop the remaining onions and place in the saucepan and cook till soft.

6. Chop the tomatoes finely or grind them in a mixer and add to the onion alongwith finely chopped apricots, the garlic slices, coriander and fresh mint, and cook till you get a thick gravy. Add the Kashmiri chillies. Cook over a slow fire for 10 minutes. Toss in the meatballs.

7. Line a dish with orange slices and lettuce leaves and place the meatballs in the centre with the apricot gravy.

8. Serve with hot rotlis.

KHIMO-SALI-VATANA-SATHE

[Mutton Mince with Green Peas and Potato Shoestrings (Sali)]

Preparation Time: 7 mins.
Cooking Time: 40 mins. • Serves 6

200 gms. potato shoestrings (sali)
200 gms. green peas
350 gms. mutton mince
2   large onions, finely chopped
$^{1}/_{2}$ cup coriander, washed chopped
4   large tomatoes skinned and finely chopped
4   green chillies, deseeded and finely chopped
1   tablespoon ginger-garlic paste
1   teaspoon turmeric
1   teaspoon Kashmiri chilli powder
2   teaspoons garam masala
$^{1}/_{2}$ teaspoon mace powder
$^{1}/_{2}$ teaspoon cumin, roasted coarsely ground
$^{1}/_{2}$ teaspoon coriander seeds, roasted
2   sour limes, juice removed
      one pinch soda bicarb
      salt
      oil

1. Place the chopped onions along with three tablespoons oil in a wide mouthed vessel. Cook the onions till they are golden in colour. Add the mince, ginger-garlic paste, salt and mix vigorously for 5 minutes. Lower the flame and add the turmeric, chilli and garam masala powders as well as the roasted cumin, coriander and mace powders. Add the chopped tomatoes, green chillies and allow to cook over a very low heat for 10 minutes. Then add four cups of water and allow to cook again over low heat till the mince is soft and tender.

2. Place four cups of water to boil, add two teaspoons salt and a pinch of soda-bicarb and boil the green peas. Cook till tender and drain. Do not overcook or the peas will separate from their skins and become mushy. Drain in a colander and add to the cooked mince along with the lime juice and chopped coriander. Stir well.

3. Serve the mince in a flat dish and decorate with the potato shoestrings (Sali).

KHIMO

(Minced Mutton)

Preparation Time: 7 mins.
Cooking Time: 40 mins. • Serves 6-9

500 gms. minced meat
2   large onions
300 gms. cubed potatoes
2   carrots chopped into dice
3   green chillies
$^{1}/_{2}$ bunch coriander
2   ripe red tomatoes
1   teaspoon turmeric
$1^{1}/_{2}$ teaspoons chilli powder
2   teaspoons sugar
2   dessertspoons vinegar
$1^{1}/_{2}$ teaspoons ginger-garlic paste
      salt
      ghee

1. Marinate the minced meat in salt and ginger-garlic paste. Cover and keep aside.

2. Chop the onions finely and fry till golden brown. Then add the spices and mince and stir till the meat is dry; add the vegetables after which put in $2^{1}/_{2}$ cups of water and allow to simmer over a low flame for 35 minutes.

3. When the water has been absorbed and the mince cooked add the chopped tomatoes, coriander, sugar and vinegar and cook for 10 minutes more. Cover and set aside.

SPECIAL GOS-NA-CUTLES

(Frilled Mutton Cutlets)

Preparation Time: 20 mins.
Cooking Time: 35 mins. • Serves 18-20

1	tablespoon ginger-garlic paste
500 gms.	mutton kheema
500 gms.	boiled potato, finely mashed
2	medium sized onions, finely chopped
$1/2$	cup coriander leaves, finely chopped
1	tablespoon green chillies, finely chopped
1	tablespoon fresh mint, finely chopped
1	tablespoon Parsi dhanajeera or dhanshak masala
1	tablespoon red chilli powder
$1^1/_2$	teaspoons turmeric powder
4-6	raw eggs
	bread crumbs
1	teaspoon garam masala
	oil for frying
	salt

1. In a large thala mix together the salt, ginger-garlic paste and the kheema and allow to stand for one hour.

2. Boil the potatoes in a pressure cooker. Skin and mash well. Add to the raw kheema and mix thoroughly. Add the onions, chillies, coriander and powdered spices. Divide into round balls according to the size of the cutlet you desire.

3. Spread bread crumbs on a wooden cutting board. Roll the meatball in the bread crumbs and flatten it out in an oval shape with a knife.

4. Heat oil in a flat frying pan. Beat 4 eggs in a bowl. Dip the cutlets in the beaten egg and carefully slip into the hot oil. Turn the cutlets only once. Remove from oil when brown in colour.

5. Serve on a bed of cabbage and lettuce surrounded by cucumber and tomatoes. Garnish with wedges of sour lime. Serve with fried chips and tomato gravy.

GOS-NA-CUTLES

(Minced Meat Cutlets)

Preparation Time: 15 mins.
Cooking Time: 30 mins. • Makes: 18-22

500 gms.	minced mutton
1	tablespoon ginger-garlic paste
2	small onions
$1/_4$	bunch coriander
1	teaspoon pepper powder
2	teaspoons chilli powder
2-4	eggs
16	slices of bread soaked in water
$1/_2$	cup bread crumbs
	salt
	ghee for deep frying

1. Salt the mince, add ginger-garlic paste, pepper and chilli powder, mix and form into a ball and keep aside. Soak bread in three cups of water.

2. Chop the onions and coriander finely; drain the water from the soaked bread and crush it to a pulp and add these three ingredients to the mince.

3. Beat the eggs stiffly and fold into the mince mixture.

4. Sprinkle the bread crumbs on a wooden board. Divide the mince into equal portions. Take each portion and pat it into an oval shape. Coat with bread crumbs on both sides and deep fry in ghee till brown.

5. These cutlets should be served hot with thick Parsi style tomato sauce.

TAM-TAMTA-GOS-NA-KABAB

(Hot Mutton Kababs)

Preparation Time: 30 mins.
Cooking Time: 35 mins. • Serves 10-12

These kababs are a MUST with dhansakh and black masoor. I use fresh turmeric instead of the dried powder. This gives it a distinct flavour. Soonamai rarely used powdered turmeric. She got her mince and masalas ground in a mortar on her back verandah.

500 gms. minced mutton
400 gms. mashed potato
2   large onions, finely chopped
$\frac{1}{2}$ cup coriander, chopped
2-3 tablespoons mint, chopped
2   tablespoons green chillies, chopped
1-2 tablespoons fresh turmeric, chopped
2   tablespoons ginger-garlic paste
1   tablespoon red chilli powder
2   tablespoons Parsi dhansakh masala
$\frac{1}{2}$ teaspoon mace or powdered javantri
4-6 eggs
     bread crumbs
     oil for frying

1. Take a large thala. Place the mince along with the ginger-garlic paste in it. Mix well and form a ball. Cover and leave till you have chopped the onions, chillies, mint, coriander and ground the fresh turmeric.

2. Mix the mince with the finely mashed potatoes, fresh and dry masalas. Add sufficient salt. Make medium sized round balls.

3. Place a kadhai with oil on a high flame. Dip the balls in beaten egg and coat with bread crumbs. Lower flame. Fry till golden brown and cooked from within.

4. Alternately you can roll the raw kababs in bread crumbs, dip in beaten egg and fry. These are best eaten fresh.

PAPAO-NI-GRAVY-MA-CUTLES

(Mutton Cutlets in Papaya Gravy)

Preparation Time: 10 mins.
Cooking Time: 20 mins. • Serves 10-12

Prepare cutlets as in recipe in this book.
For the Papaya Gravy
1   medium sized ripe papaya
6   Kashmiri chillies   ⎫
$\frac{1}{2}$" piece fresh turmeric   ⎬ grind well
$\frac{1}{2}$" piece fresh ginger   │ with lime
$\frac{1}{2}$ teaspoon cumin seeds   ⎭ juice
2   tablespoons fresh chopped coriander
2   tablespoons sugar
1   large onion
1   large tomato
1   cup tomato sauce
1   sour lime, juice removed
     salt
     oil

1. Skin papaya, deseed and cut the flesh into large pieces.

2. Grind the spices with the lime juice and then grind the onion and tomato to a pulp.

3. Place two tablespoons of oil in a saucepan or vessel. Heat and fry the ground masala and add the onion and tomato pulp and fry for 5 minutes till red. Put in the papaya pieces, salt to taste and half a cup of water and shake the vessel from side to side and allow to simmer for 10 minutes. Taste for salt. Add the tomato sauce.

4. Serve the hot gravy over freshly fried cutlets, or serve separately, as desired. Garnish with coriander leaves.

MAIJI NA LACH-LACH TA KAJU MA KOFTA

(Delicious Koftas in Kaju Gravy)

Preparation Time: 40 mins.
Cooking Time: 45-50 mins. • Serves 4-6

500 gms. minced meat
1 tablespoon ginger-garlic paste
1 large onion finely chopped
$\frac{1}{2}$ bunch finely chopped
  coriander
6 green chillies deseeded &
  finely chopped
1 teaspoon red chilli powder
1 teaspoon mace powder
1 teaspoon black pepper, cloves
  and cinnamon powder
4 raw eggs
$\frac{1}{4}$ cup channa ata
salt to taste
peanut oil

> for the koftas

thick milk from half a grated
coconut
3 bay leaves
200 gms. kaju paste
$\frac{1}{2}$ tablespoon ground aniseed
$\frac{1}{2}$ teaspoon cumin seeds
1 cup thick curd whisked with
  1 tablespoon sugar
2 tablespoons coriander finely chopped
  salt
  groundnut oil

> for the gravy

1. Mix the mince with all the powdered masala, chana ata, eggs and the ginger-garlic paste. If possible grind it in a stone quern or liquidizer. Add salt to taste and mix in the finely chopped onions, green chillies and coriander. Make round balls and keep aside.

2. Take a large flat bottomed vessel and pour in half a cup of oil. Fry the kaju paste, bay leaves, cumin seeds and ground aniseeds, very lightly over a medium flame for a few minutes. Add the thick coconut milk and stir and cook the gravy over a low fire for seven minutes till it boils.

3. Gently place all the koftas into the pan and do not touch them with a spoon or spatula. Hold the vessels in both hands with thick tea towels and sway the vessel back and forth till all the koftas are covered with the gravy. If necessary add half a cup of water. Cook covered for 15 minutes on a medium flame till the koftas are cooked through.

4. Just before serving heat again, sprinkle with the chopped coriander and drop tablespoons of the whisked curd on top. Eat with parathas or vegetable khichdi or pulao.

MASALA-NA-CHAAP

(Savoury Mutton Chops)

Preparation Time: 4 hours.
Cooking Time: 2 hours. • Serves 10-12

18 double chops
2   onions sliced
1" piece of ginger finely ground
1   teaspoon black pepper powder
1/2 cup thick curd
    one pinch of saffron
    ghee

1. Wash and salt the chops and mix in the ginger paste, the black pepper powder and heated saffron. Allow to marinate for four hours.

2. Take half a cup of ghee and heat in a flat bottomed vessel. When hot place the chops at the bottom of the vessel and turn quickly to seal the chops. You will need to do this in two to three batches. Use more ghee if you need.

3. Place all the chops together with the onions in the same vessel over a very slow fire. Add one cup of water at a time and cook them till soft, turning them every 15 minutes or so. This will take two hours.

4. When the chops soften, whisk the curd and pour over the chops.

5. Cook for another half an hour till the curd has dried.

DODHI-YA-KAKRI-NI-BURIYANI

(White Gourd or Large Cucumbers Cooked in Mutton Gravy)

Preparation Time: 35 mins.
Cooking Time: 45 mins. • Serves 6-8

500 gms. leg mutton chunks with nali
500 gms. skinned white gourd or skinned large
        cucumbers with the seeds removed
2   onions sliced and deep fried
2   onions finely chopped
4   large tomatoes skinned, deseeded and finely
        chopped
6   Kashmiri chillies or
7   green chillies   } grind
1   tablespoon cumin seeds   together
1   pod garlic   in a little
1   teaspoon black peppercorns water
3   tablespoons coriander, chopped
    salt
    oil

1. Wash and apply salt to the mutton and cook in a pressure cooker with three cups water till the mutton is tender.

2. Cut the cucumber or white gourd into cubes, salt it and cook in a pressure cooker in one and a half cup of water till soft. Mash the vegetable.

3. Heat the onions in half a cup of oil and when pink add the ground masala and fry over a low flame till red. Add the tomatoes and cook till soft. Add the mutton pieces and mix well with the masala. Add the mashed vegetables and stir. Then pour in two cups of the mutton soup left in the pressure cooker. Simmer for 15 minutes and serve covered with the fried onions and freshly chopped coriander.

4. Parsis normally eat this gravied vegetable and meat with white rice.

BADAMI CURRY

(Almond Curry)

Preparation Time: 35-40 mins.
Cooking Time: 30 mins. • Serves 8-10

2   large coconuts, milk removed
1 kg. mutton chunks
30-40 boiled peeled almonds
2½ tablespoons whole dhania
     or coriander seeds
1   tablespoon poppy seeds
1   tablespoon sesame seeds
¼   nutmeg
2   large onions, chopped   } broil lightly, grind with half a cup of water
2   large tomatoes, chopped
4   deseeded green chillies
10   Kashmiri chillies
15   cloves garlic
2   green cardamoms
1"   piece fresh ginger
1"   piece fresh turmeric
2   tablespoons gram flour
     salt
     refined oil

1. Grind all the masalas to a soft paste with half a cup of water. Grind the almonds separately on a mortar.

2. Cook the meat with salt and four cups of water in a pressure cooker till tender. Keep mutton pieces and the soup in separate vessels.

3. Heat half a cup of oil and fry the ground masala and gram flour till red for five minutes. Add mutton, two cups of the mutton soup and the thick coconut milk. Allow to simmer for twenty minutes. Taste for salt and serve with plain white rice.

GOS-NI-KARI

(Mutton Curry)

Preparation Time: 30 mins.
Cooking Time: 40 mins. • Serves 10

1   kg. leg mutton chunks with nali
250 gms. potatoes, peeled, cut
200 gms. onions, finely chopped
3   tablespoons gram flour
1   coconut, grated
16   Kashmiri red chillies
75   gms. coriander seeds
25   gms. khaskhas or poppy seeds
25   gms. sesame seeds
1"   piece ginger   } grind together
20   cloves garlic
100 gms. cashewnuts
10   black peppercorns
1   small lime sized knob tamarind
1   green cardamom crushed
1   teaspoon turmeric powder
1   sprig curry leaves
1   cup oil
     salt

1. Wash the meat and potatoes well and place them along with two teaspoons coarse salt and four tea cups of water in a pressure cooker and cook till soft.

2. Grind the masala till soft. Place the finely chopped onions in a vessel along with half cup refined oil. When the onion becomes pink add the curry leaves, turmeric, cardamom and the gram flour and fry well. After two minutes add the masala, lower the flame and allow to cook for five minutes till red.

3. Strain the soup through a fine sieve into the masala and then add the mutton and potato pieces. Stir and allow to simmer for 25 minutes before serving. Taste for salt.

AIMAI NO LEELO RAS

(Aimai's Green Nergisi Kofta Curry)

Preparation Time: 45 mins.
Cooking Time: 50 mins. • Serves 6

For the Koftas
4   boiled eggs halved
300 gms. minced meat
$\frac{1}{2}$ teaspoon ground ginger-garlic paste
1   large onion finely chopped
3   green chillies, deseeded and finely chopped
$\frac{1}{2}$ cup coriander, chopped
$\frac{1}{2}$ teaspoon black pepper, cloves and cinnamon powder
2   eggs whisked
1   tablespoon mint, chopped
     salt to taste

For the Curry
1   coconut, freshly grated
2   cups coriander, chopped
6   green chillies, finely chopped
1   tablespoon mint, chopped
3   tablespoons gram flour
1   large onion, grated
1   tablespoon khaskhas or poppy seeds
1   tablespoon til
1   tablespoon dhania or dry coriander seeds
} grind together
2   sour limes, juice removed
     curry leaves
$\frac{1}{2}$ - 1 cup til oil

1. Grind finely all the spices, onion, green coriander and chillies on a mortar till a smooth paste is acquired.

2. Heat $\frac{1}{2}$ cup til oil. Add the curry leaves and stir briskly. Add the green coconut masala. Lower heat and keep stirring. Add salt and the desired amount of water and allow to simmer.

3. Whilst the curry is simmering take a thali and place the mince on it. Add salt, powdered masala, ground ginger-garlic, chopped onion, chillies, mint and coriander. Mix well and form a smooth ball.

4. Whisk the eggs. Make a hole in the centre of the mince ball and slowly mix into the mince until all the egg is absorbed.

5. Divide the mixture into 8 parts. Wet your hands and make a flat circle of each portion of mince in the palm of your left hand. Place a halved, boiled egg onto the mixture and enfold it in the mince. Shape to look like an egg.

6. When all the koftas have been made, increase the heat of the stove on which the curry is simmering and drop the koftas one by one into the boiling gravy. Allow to boil for 7-12 minutes. Shake the vessel back and forth. When cooked, remove the vessel from the stove, add the sour lime juice and serve with boiled white rice and pappadums.

87

RICE

Parsis love to eat rice. It is the staple food along with rice rotlis in the villages of Gujarat. Normally it is the fat rice grain which is cooked daily for the lunch meal. It is served with pink lentil gravy, a coconut curry, minced meat or yoghurt curry with bhajias. The poorest of the poor would boil the rice they received as their daily wages from the farmers or landlady, with a lot of water. They would add a pinch of salt, a chilli or two and when the rice was mushy and soft, they would drain the liquid leftover into a terracotta pot and drink the thick soup called 'page' before they ate the rice with small bits of raw onion, chillies and occasionally roasted dried fish.

In the houses of the landed Parsis, it is different, although if we compare their lives to ours today, they seem to have lived like Spartans.

Since water was scarce and had to be carried from a common well outside the family premises, all vegetables grown were dependent upon the rains. They learnt to dehydrate their vegetables in order to store them for the monsoon season. Chillies, coriander, pumpkins, squash and cucumbers were chopped, dried in the sun and preserved. The same was done with fish. Thousands of Bombay Ducks were dried on rooftop along with filleted surmai, ghol and dahara fish.

As a rule the afternoon rice meal was accompanied by mango pickle called "methioo", the recipe is in this book. My great-grandmother Soonamai usually got a Brahmin Hindu family to make the years supply for her in exchange for paddy.

The fine, home grown "Kolam" rice was reserved for feast and happy occasions.

At the present time — half a century later — Parsis still eat rice mainly in the afternoons. At night, they eat bread or wheat rotlis. They love their rice cooked as "Khichdi" and "pulaos".

SADO GOS-NO-PULAO

(Simple Mutton Pulao)

Preparation Time: 15 mins.
Cooking Time: 45 mins. • Serves 6-8

300 gms.	mutton pieces
300 gms.	basmati rice
4	large onions
1	tablespoon ginger-garlic paste
2-3	tablespoons garam masala (powdered cloves, cinnamon, black pepper and cardamom)
3	bay leaves
2	badian
2	black elchas
1	teaspoon Kashmiri chilli powder
5	large potatoes cubed and fried
	ghee
	salt to taste

1. Wash the rice and set aside.

2. Slice all the onions finely. Deep fry half and set aside. In a large vessel fry the remaining onions in half cup ghee. When golden brown add the bay leaves, badian, elcha and the washed rice. Stir, add two litres water and cook till rice is tender and fluffy. Rice is best cooked in an electric rice cooker.

3. Meanwhile, place half a cup of ghee in a pressure cooker and when hot fry the meat in it till red. Add the salt, garam masala, chilli powder and ginger-garlic paste. Fry well, scraping the bottom of the cooker. Add water 2-3 cups and cook till tender.

4. Make layers of rice, meat and potatoes in a dekchi. Seal it tightly with foil or dough and place over a low heat for 15 minutes.

5. Serve sprinkled with the reserved deep fried onions.

BADSHAHI KESRI PULAO

(Emperor's Mutton Pulao)

Preparation Time: 2¹/₂ hrs.
Cooking Time: 1 hr. 15 mins. • Serves 8-10

1	kg. mutton cut into chunks
500	gms. basmati rice
2	gms saffron
4	silver leaves or vark
300	gms. thick curd
2	large onions, finely sliced
2	large onions, finely chopped
4	large tomatoes, finely chopped
4	large potatoes, skinned and cubed

1" piece cinnamon
1   teaspoon shahjeera
1   badian
3   cloves
12 black peppercorns
4-6 Kashmiri chillies   } grind
1   teaspoon cardamom and   together
    nutmeg powder
1   teaspoon badisonf or fennel
2   tablespoons each fresh
    coriander and mint

4   bay leaves
1¹/₂ tablespoon ginger-garlic paste
1   cup wheat flour
    salt
    oil or ghee

1. Wash the chopped meat, apply salt and marinate in the ginger-garlic paste.

2. Grind all the spices in a mixer.

3. Heat the saffron on an iron skillet till crisp. Crumble between your finger tips, add to the curd and whip it lightly. Add the spices and the curd to the meat. Keep in a cool place for two hours.

4. After two hours heat half cup oil in a pressure cooker and put chopped onions. When they become red-brown, add the mutton mixture and allow to sizzle. Cook for five to seven minutes, add two to three cups of water and the tomatoes, close the cooker. Cook the mutton till soft.

5. Fry the sliced onions till golden brown, then the cubed potatoes and set aside.

6. Boil the rice and bay leaves in salted water and strain through a colander before it becomes soft.

7. Take a large dekchi with a fitting lid. Place some oil about a quarter cup at the bottom. Then place a layer of rice at the bottom of the vessel. Then a layer of mutton on top. Spread some potatoes on the meat. Make these layers till all your rice, meat and potatoes are covered. Sprinkle on top sliced onions and cover with the lid. Cover with the silver pieces.

8. Knead the flour with a little water till you get a thick dough. Roll out into a thick rope and place it on the lid and pinch it along the rim so that the lid is firmly attached to the vessel. Then place the dekchi on a very low flame for half an hour.

9. When you are ready to eat, remove the wheat dough and serve the pulao with kachumber and if preferred with dhansakh dal.

DUMBO-MARGHI-PULAO BHARELO

(Lamb Stuffed with Chicken Pulao and Roasted)

Preparation Time: 3 hours
Cooking Time: 6 hours. • Serves 50

1	whole lamb roughly about 8 kgs. in weight
5	gms. saffron
2	kgs. chicken pulao with dried fruits (see page 96)
12	boiled eggs, halved
3	kgs. yoghurt
4	tablespoons ginger-garlic paste
4	tablespoons garam masala
2	tablespoons black peppercorns, coarsely ground
2	tablespoons tenderiser
5	kgs. pure ghee
	salt
	oil

1. You can leave the head of the lamb on or get it chopped off. I prefer the latter. Get your butcher to clean the lamb well. Wash it inside and out twice.

2. Make the chicken pulao as given in this book. Use 5 gms. of saffron in the rice and stuff the lamb with all the boiled eggs. Sew up the stomach and neck cavity with a large needle and thick white thread.

3. Poke the lamb all over with the tines of a fork. Apply salt, yoghurt, garam masala, black peppercorn, ginger-garlic paste and tenderiser. Allow to marinate for two hours or longer.

4. Take a huge dekchi or Langri and heat it over a coal fire. Put in 3 kgs. ghee and place the lamb in the hot ghee and after it has become red brown turn over on the other side, add the remaining ghee and cook over a steady low flame. Add 2 litres of water at a time. Cover and cook

over a medium flame. Keep adding water as it dries up and cook over a low coal fire till the meat is soft and tender. This will take between 4-6 hours.

SOONAMAI-NO-KERI-NO PULAO

(Soonamai's Mango Pulao)

Preparation Time: 2$\frac{1}{2}$ hrs.
Cooking Time: 2$\frac{1}{2}$ hrs. • Serves 6-8

6	large ripe alphonso mangoes
300	gms. boneless mutton cubes
400	gms. basmati rice
10	black peppercorns
3	medium onions
2	teaspoons garam masala
$\frac{1}{2}$	teaspoon mace powder
$\frac{1}{2}$	teaspoon nutmeg-cardamom powder
2	bay leaves
1	teaspoon sugar
1$\frac{1}{2}$	teaspoon ginger-garlic paste
	salt
	ghee

1. Wash the mutton and marinate for half an hour in salt and ginger-garlic paste. Chop two onions finely and fry along with two tablespoons of ghee in a vessel over medium flame. When the onions turn golden add the peppercorns, mutton powdered masalas and cook the meat for 10 minutes in its own juices. Add four teacups water and allow to cook till tender over a very low flame. This will take at least two hours.

2. Slice the remaining onion and fry in a large pan in four tablespoons of ghee. Wash the rice and add to the pan. Fry along with the onion for five minutes. Add water till it comes one inch above the rice. Add salt, bay leaves and cook on

high heat till the water boils. Cover and cook over very low heat till the rice is soft. Run a fork through it so it becomes fluffy and loose.

3. Peel the mangoes. Cut the cheeks from both sides and run a vertical knife so you get two large pieces. Cut each into three pieces. Cut thin strips from both sides of the seed and cut each into three pieces. Place in a glass bowl and sprinkle sugar over the pieces. Mix, cover and place in the refrigerator.

4. When the mutton is cooking the water will evaporate so keep adding an extra cup of warm water at a time till the mutton disintegrates when you pinch it. One cup of gravy should remain when done.

5. Place the mango pieces in a small vessel and heat over a low fire five minutes before you serve your meal. Empty the warm rice on a platter, spread over the boiling mutton and gravy. Top with hot mango pieces and serve immediately.

LEHZAT WALLO PULAO
(Delicious Aromatic Pulao)

Preparation Time: 1 hr.
Cooking Time: 3$\frac{1}{2}$ hrs • Serves 8-10

2	gms. saffron
500	gms. basmati rice
400	gms. mutton pieces
350	gms. potatoes
300	gms. sliced onions, deep fried
200	gms. thick curd
4-8	green chillies
1	tablespoon mace or javantri
1	tablespoon shahjeera
1	tablespoon black peppercorns
$\frac{1}{2}$	tablespoon cinnamon
$\frac{1}{2}$	teaspoon cloves
$\frac{1}{2}$	teaspoon cardamom
$\frac{1}{2}$	nutmeg
8	Kashmiri chillies
2	tablespoons ginger-garlic paste
200	gms. almonds
200	gms. kismis
4	bay leaves
	foil
	salt
	ghee

(mace, shahjeera, black peppercorns, cinnamon, cloves, cardamom, nutmeg) coarsely ground

1. Wash the basmati rice twice. Take a large vessel half full of water and set it to heat. When the water starts bubbling add salt to taste, two tablespoons ghee and the four bay leaves. Allow the rice to par boil, it should not be completely cooked but hard. Strain the water through a colander and spread it on a large thali. Grate the nutmeg on top of the rice.

2. Grind the spices coarsely. Deep fry the finely sliced onions. Cut potatoes into cubes, apply salt and deep fry them and set aside. Wash and fry the almonds after boiling. Wash and fry the kismis.

3. Wash the mutton well. Salt it and marinate in the ginger-garlic paste.

4. Take two cups of ghee and place in a large, heavy bottomed dekchi. Allow to heat and add the whole Kashmiri chillies, mutton and cook till red. Lower the flame, add three to four cups of water and allow to cook till soft. Keep adding water as needed till the mutton is soft. Cover the mutton with a heavy lid and place some water on the lid also.

5. Mix the ground masala and the fried onions in the rice. Whip the curd with a pinch of sugar. When the meat is tender and soft, mix in the whipped curd. Heat the saffron on a tava and mix it in a cup of hot water. Allow to steep for one hour, before cooking the rice or meat. Sprinkle the saffron water over the half cooked rice.

6. Take a nice dekchi with a heavy bottom. Smear one cup of ghee on the bottom and sides of the dekchi and place a layer of saffron rice on it. Spread some fried onions and potatoes on the rice and a few almond slices and kismis. Then keep making rice and mutton layers till both the items are used up. Take a heavy lid and cover the dekchi and use foil to double close the lid tightly.

7. Place over a low coal sigri and place some hot coals on the lid also. Cook in this manner for two to three hours before serving the pulao. No water should be poured over the rice before it is covered. The rice should cook in the mutton soup itself. So never allow the mutton to dry out completely for a pulao which is cooked on dum.

8. Serve with kachumber.

KHEEMA MALAI PULAO

(Mince Pulao with Cream)

Preparation Time: 50 mins.
Cooking Time: 1 hr. • Serves 6-8

I love experimenting with food and this is a rice dish which can be eaten on it's own. Its luscious and needs no dal or gravy accompaniment.

300 gms. mince meat
400 gms. basmati rice
1/2 teaspoon jelabi colour
2 bay leaves
2 cups thick fresh curd
2 onions, sliced and fried
2 onions, chopped
2 large tomatoes, chopped
1 teaspoon fennel seeds
1 teaspoon mace
1 teaspoon shahjeera
1 star anise
7 Kashmiri red chillies
10 peppercorns
1" piece cinnamon
2 green cardamoms
1/2 teaspoon nutmeg powder
2 green chillies
1/2 cup fresh coriander leaves
1 tablespoon fresh mint leaves
6 boiled eggs
2 tablespoons sugar
2 tablespoons ginger-garlic paste
2 tablespoons black currants, fried
  salt
  refined oil or pure ghee

} grind together for the mince in 1/4 cup water

1. Divide the rice into 2 portions, boil one in salted water along with one bay leaf. Drain when soft. Boil the other portion in salted water along with the one bay leaf and the jelabi colour. Drain when soft. Melt half cup ghee and pour over both the rice.

2. Grind the mince masala till soft.

3. Place the chopped onions in half a cup oil in a large pan and cook till soft. Let it

turn golden brown and add the masala and fry till red. Lower flame and when the oil leaves the masala add the mince, ginger-garlic paste and salt and mix thoroughly. Add the chopped tomatoes and cook over a very slow fire till dry. Add 1 cup of water and cook slowly till the mince is tender. If necessary add more water, the mince must be very soft.

4. Place half the rice in an aluminium baking tray. Spread all the hot kheema over the rice evenly. Then spread the yellow rice over it. Decorate with sliced boiled eggs, fried black currants and the fried sliced onions. Whip the curd with the sugar and spread over the top. Serve immediately.

MAMMA NO SIMLA MARCHA BHARELO PULAO

(Mamma's Stuffed Capsicum Pulao)

Preparation Time: 40-45 mins.
Cooking Time: 1 hr. 15 mins. • Serves 10-12

My mother is a great cook and she learnt everything from my grandmother Cooverbai. But how she got onto this particular recipe I don't know. I think she once ate this dish at her friend Aloo Batliboi's house.

One large capsicum is enough for each person, but at a party, for say ten people, you should cook at least fifteen of them.

15 large capsicums
$^1/_2$ kg. mince cooked exactly as for mutton pattice filling
450 gms. basmati rice
4 large tomatoes
3 large onions
3 bay leaves
1 teaspoon coarsely ground shahjeera
1" piece cinnamon
1 teaspoon mace powder
2 crushed cardamoms
4 cloves
2 cups sweet curds. The amount is up to you
1 tablespoon sugar
    oil
    salt to taste

1. Chop the onions in slices, and slowly cook them in one cup ghee. Add the whole spices and washed rice and cook till soft. The rice should not be lumpy, or soggy or spongy. Spread it out on a large thali.

2. Wash the capsicums, remove seeds and the stalks carefully by keeping some of the capsicums attached to the stalk, as you will need it to act as a cover for the stuffed capsicum.

3. Stuff all the capsicums carefully with the mince and recap with the stalk covers.

4. Take a wide mouthed vessel and arrange the capsicums in circles so they do not over balance. Pour some oil in the dekchi from the sides. Cover and cook over a slow fire and keep adding a little water and fine salt as needed. The capsicums have to be soft. If you don't cook them properly, the taste and pleasure in eating the dish will be lost.

5. Chop the tomatoes finely after skinning and deseeding them. Mix in the sugar, coarsely ground shahajeera and the mace powder. Add beaten curds. Sprinkle this mixture on the rice. Mix carefully so the rice is not broken.

6. Grease the bottom of a large flat vessel with oil. Spread some of the rice mixture on its base and make 15 holes. Place the capsicums in the holes and cover almost all the way upto the top with rice. Do not cover the capsicums. The tops and the stalks should be seen. Cover the vessel.

7. Place the vessel on top of another large vessel half full of water. Allow the water to boil and cook the dish in its steam for half an hour.

8. Serve hot with dhansakh dal.

This unusual dish is a great favourite with my family because, it is cooked so rarely. However, my brother, Sohraab is allergic to capsicums. So be careful when you serve it at parties.

FRENY-NO-KOFTA-NO-PULAO

(Freny's Meatball Pulao)

Preparation Time: 40-45 mins.
Cooking Time: 40-50 mins. • Serves 6-8

300 gms. raw mince
500 gms. long grained rice
1 tablespoon ginger-garlic paste
6 large onions
4 large tomatoes
10 large green chillies
1/4 bunch coriander
1 tablespoon chilli powder
1/2 teaspoon turmeric powder
1/2 teaspoon pepper powder
3 tablespoons Parsi dhansakh masala
1 tablespoon sugar
3 lemons juice, removed
2 eggs
3 bay leaves
1 teaspoon javantri & nutmeg powder
oil
salt to taste

1. Wash the rice and cook with one tablespoon ghee, bay leaves and salt to taste, in the usual way till the grains are separated.

2. To the mince add the salt, pepper, ginger-garlic paste, six finely chopped green chillies, half of the finely chopped coriander and Parsi dhansakh masala. Mix thoroughly, form into a ball, cover and keep aside.

3. Chop the onions. Skin and chop the tomatoes and cook both in four tablespoons of ghee. After the tomatoes have softened add salt, the remaining four green chillies finely chopped, the chilli and turmeric powders and two cups water. Stir till the gravy becomes smooth. When the gravy begins to boil add the javantri and nutmeg powder.

4. When the tomato gravy shows signs of thickening add the beaten eggs to the mince and mix thoroughly and then form small balls. Wet hands frequently so that the meat does not adhere to them and drop one by one into the boiling tomato gravy. Cover and cook over a low flame. Do not stir with a spoon but shake the vessel from side to side. Add the lemon juice and sugar once the meat-balls are cooked. Mix the gravy gently with the cooked rice and sprinkle with the remainder of the finely chopped coriander.

5. Alternately layer the pulao and serve sprinkled with the coriander.

NARGOLIO-KOLMI-NO-PULAO

(Delicious prawn pulao from Nargol)

Preparation Time: 50 mins.
Cooking Time: 45 mins. • Serves 4-6

350 gms. basmati rice
30-40 large prawns, shelled, deveined
4   large onions, chopped
1   cup fried onions
500 gms. large red tomatoes, deseeded
2   gms. saffron
2   coarse thick lemon grass stalks
$^{1}/_{2}$ cup chopped coriander
7   green chillies fresh
7   red Kashmiri chillies
16   black peppercorns
1   tablespoon cumin seeds
1   tablespoon fennel seeds   to grind
1"   fresh ginger — sliced   together
1   pod garlic
2   cardamoms
1   teaspoon fresh turmeric
2   stems curry leaves
      salt
      ghee

1. Boil the rice in a large pan of salted water. Pound the lemon grass and add it to the rice. When soft, strain the rice in a colander and remove the lemon grass.

2. Heat the saffron gently on an iron skillet and when crisp, crumble with your finger tips on the boiled rice. Fluff the rice so the saffron is well mixed.

3. Wash prawns, salt and set aside.

4. Grind the masalas into a fine paste with the help of a little water.

5. Place the large onions in a heavy based vessel. Add half cup ghee and cook till golden. Add the masala. Skin tomatoes, chop finely and add to the masala along with the curry leaves. Add the prawns, cover and cook for 15 minutes over a low fire. Add water and salt if necessary. Cook till the prawns are tender. Add coriander.

6. Arrange the rice and prawn mixture in layers in two pyrex bowls and top with the fried onions.

TATRELI MARGHI-NO-PULAO

(Savoury Chicken Pulao)

Preparation Time: 25 mins.
Cooking Time: 40-50 mins. • Serves 4-6

1	medium sized tender chicken
2	teaspoons ginger-garlic paste
300 gms.	basmati rice
4	large onions
4	large potatoes
3	large tomatoes
200 gms.	curd
10	big Kashmiri chillies
10	peppercorns
2"	cinnamon sticks
3	cloves
$1/2$	teaspoon mace powder
$1/2$	teaspoon shahjeera powder
100 gms.	cashewnuts, fried
4	hard boiled eggs
	saffron or jelabi colour
	ghee
	salt to taste

1. Clean the chicken and cut into eight small pieces. Wash thoroughly, apply salt and ginger-garlic paste and keep aside.

2. Make into powder the red chillies, peppercorns, cloves, cinnamon. Whip the curd and mix together with all the spices and then pour over the salted chicken. Cover and keep for at least two hours.

3. Whilst the chicken is being marinated, peel the onions and potatoes; cut two onions horizontally and slice thinly. Chop the remaining two onions and keep aside. Cut the potatoes into eight pieces each.

4. Salt the potatoes, deep fry to a golden colour and drain. In the same ghee fry the two sliced onions until crisp. Keep both the onions and potatoes aside.

5. Wash the rice, add salt to taste and cook with slightly less water than usual.

6. Fry the chopped onions till brown in three tablespoons of the left over ghee from the fried potatoes and onions.

7. Chop the tomatoes finely and add to the browned onions. When a slight gravy forms, toss in the marinated chicken and cook over a medium heat till the meat turns red. Add the mace and shahjeera powder. Add two cups water and cook over a slow heat till tender.

8. Take a deep, large-mouthed vessel and spread an alternate layer of rice, fried onion and potato and chicken till both rice and chicken are used up. With the end of a knife bore five holes from the top of the rice to the bottom of the vessel and pour in the remainder of the chicken gravy. Soak one teaspoon of saffron in four dessertspoons of hot water. Mix thoroughly and pour over the rice.

9. Cover the vessel and put into an oven 300°F or on dum (low heat) for one to two hours.

10. Serve decorated with the fried cashewnuts, sliced hard-boiled eggs. This pulao may be accompanied with Dahi-ni-Kachumber or dhansakh dal.

MACCHI-NE-TAMBOTA-NO PULAO

(Fish Pulao with Tomatoes)

Preparation Time: 40 mins.
Cooking Time: 45 mins. • Serves 6-8

12 thick fish fillets
1 cup lady fingers
1 kg. large red tomatoes
2 tablespoons sugar
500 gms Basmati rice
3 bay leaves
5 black peppercorns
1 cup chopped coriander
7 green chillies
1 pod garlic
2 tablespoon cumin
1 teaspoon mustard seeds   } grind
1 teaspoon coriander   together
  powdered
2 large onions chopped
2 teaspoons chilli powder
1 teaspoon oregano
4 boiled eggs
  salt
  ghee

Note: For fish fillets, the first preference would be rawas, then pomfret and lastly ghol fish or surmai.

1. Cook the rice in a large pan of salted water to which add 3 tablespoons of ghee, the bay leaves and peppercorns. When soft strain the rice through a colander and sprinkle half the coriander.

2. Grind the masalas with the help of a quarter cup water. Set aside.

3. Wash the tomatoes, skin and deseed. Add one cup water and liquidise to a pulp.

4. Cut the lady fingers finely, apply salt and deep fry till crisp. Place one cup of ghee in a large, heavy based fry pan. Wash and salt the fish fillets and fry very lightly on both sides in small batches and set aside. It does not matter if they are slightly raw. Put the ghee left in the pan on top of the cooked rice.

5. Take a heavy bottomed vessel. Place one cup of ghee in it and fry the masala well till it gives off a delicious aroma. Spread the masala evenly over the bottom of the vessel and place the half fried fillets on top. Lower the flame and slowly cook the fish turning the fillets once or twice. Add the tomato pulp, oregano, sugar and salt to taste. Shake the pan from side to side. Cover the vessel and simmer till a thick gravy remains. Sprinkle the gravy with the remaining coriander.

6. Take a rectangular oven dish. Place half the rice at the bottom and cover with the fish gravy. Top with the remaining rice and sliced boiled eggs. Sprinkle the fried lady fingers on top. You can heat this pulao in the oven for ten minutes before serving.

VEGETARIAN FOOD

There is one month in the Parsi calendar year when all Zoroastrians do not eat meat and poultry. It is the Boman Mahina. The angel Boman was in charge of all animal life and in order to show respect to him the majority of Zoroastrians even today do not eat flesh food on four days of this special month, Bahmon, Mor, Gos and Ram Roj. Strangely enough, the Parsis eat eggs, fish and crustaceans and still call themselves vegetarians!

In my grandmother's house, the whole month was spent eating egg, fish and vegetable dishes. The most popular vegetarian dish was made of special cooking bananas, which when fried were sweet and delicious and got caramelized in the hot ghee. The children literally waited with bated breath for their share of these golden brown, fat, juicy slices. Pulses and lentils were eaten in much more quantities than in other months and tittori was an item that was especially cooked on any one of the special four days. My paternal grandmother was very fond of double beans. They tasted like butter when cooked in a pressure cooker. To this day I cook double beans at home and even grow them in my garden in Lonavla.

During the Boman month, my mother used to make mounds of colocasia rolls which we call "patrel" and these were given as gifts to relatives and friends. I have included the recipe of these sweet, sour and hot rolls, which were sliced and deep fried and served with wedges of lime. For buffet parties we temper them with fried cumin, whole coriander seeds, whole fried kashmiri chillies and sprinkle freshly grated coconut and green coriander on top.

Field beans or papri is cooked in various ways. One forgotten method I had seen as a small child in Gujarat. A huge hole was dug in the ground and a fire was made with cowdung cakes, khajuri twigs and wooden pieces. Then mutton and chicken chunks were marinated in green chilli and garlic-ginger ground masala. Papri was cleaned and washed along with tiny brinjals and sweet potatoes and it was all arranged in layers in a large earthen clay pot. Oil was poured over it and the top was sealed with another small clay pot and the whole pot was buried underground and allowed to cook for a day and a night. Most people made only a vegetarian dish and it was called "umberiyu". Rich people added meat and chicken to it. Somehow, I didn't think the smoky taste was all that great, but most people raved about it. This item is now a thing of the past and one just does not hear about it anymore.

The other recipe which has been totally forgotten in the frenzy of Bombay city life is the Toovar Dal Pulao which I have written in detail and called Golden Bead Pulao. Parsis were so pernickaty in their food habits a hundred years ago that it passes all belief. My father-in-law used to tell us about a very rich man called Dhunjibhoy Bomanji who went to have a Dhansakh Picnic with his friends on the island of Uran, off Bombay. His cooks had forgotten to bring sour limes which we Parsis squeeze generously on the Dhansakh. Would you believe it? The launch was sent back all the way to Bombay to get the forgotten sour limes!!

PATREL

(Colocasia Savoury Rolls)

Preparation Time: Indefinite
Cooking Time: 40-45 mins. • Makes 6-8 Rolls

48	colocasia leaves
750 gms.	gram flour
4	large onions finely chopped
2	bunches fresh coriander finely chopped
1	large pod garlic
16	kashmiri chillies
15	green chillies
1	tablespoon cumin seeds
1½	tablespoon dhansakh masala
1½	tablespoon chilli powder
12	tablespoon turmeric powder
2	cups tamarind pulp
1	cup grated jaggery
	vinegar
	salt
	sesame oil

} grind in vinegar

1. Cut the stems of the colocasia leaves, wash and dry them with a soft mulmul cloth.

2. Grind the garlic, cumin, red and green chillies and powdered spices in a quarter cup of vinegar. Chop onions and coriander finely. Mix grated jaggery and tamarind pulp.

3. Seive the flour in a large thala, add salt and the ground masala, jaggery and tamarind pulp and mix well together. Add one cup of water and mix dough well. Cover and allow to stand for two hours.

4. After two hours mix the chopped onion and coriander in the gram flour. Place a huge double length newspaper on the floor or table. Weigh it down at the four corners. Place a large leaf upside down on it, take a handful of the batter and apply on the leaf. Place another leaf so that it overlaps one side of the first one and apply batter on it. Keep arranging the leaves in such a manner that you have a large square of batter filled leaves. Fold all four sides slightly inwards and roll neatly. Tie with soft white string. You should get six to eight such rolls.

5. Heat two cups sesame oil in a heavy based pan and fry the rolls gently on all sides. Add one cup water and allow to simmer. Cover the vessel tightly so that the rolls cook in the steam. Turn over the rolls and add more water if you feel necessary and keep on the stove till cooked. Cool and store in plastic bags and refrigerate.

6. When needed cut into slices and fry in hot oil and temper with mustard seeds, cumin seeds and red chillies. Serve with sour lime wedges.

SURTI-PAPRI-NU-UNDHIOO

(Surti Bean Casserole)

Preparation Time: 1-1½ hours
Cooking Time: 1-1½ hrs. • Serves 15-20

A heavy traditional medley of beans, vegetables and bananas in green tangy masala and ghee gravy. For a party of 15-20 persons you will need the following items:

500 gms. field beans or papri
150 gms. baby brinjals
150 gms. tiny tendli
150 gms. purple kamodio kand or yam
150 gms. sweet potatoes
100 gms. yam or souran
100 gms. papri seeds (beans)
8   large sweet bananas or better still raw panchdhari bananas each washed and cut into 4-6 pieces

For the masala:
½   grated coconut
10   green chillies deseeded
1½   tablespoons ginger, chopped
1½   tablespoons garlic, chopped
15   black peppercorns
1"   piece cinnamon
6   cloves   }
3   green cardamoms   } grind
¼   nutmeg   } together
2   tablespoons cumin seeds
1   tablespoon sesame seeds
1   teaspoon mustard seeds
1   cup fresh coriander, finely chopped
1   teaspoon ajwain seeds
2   teaspoons turmeric powder
2   teaspoons sambhar masala
1   teaspoon asafoetida
2   sprigs curry leaves
a pinch of cooking soda or baking powder

For the muthias:
150 gms gram flour
1   small onion finely chopped
1   bunch fenugreek spinach large leaves juice of two limes
2   teaspoons sugar

one pinch soda-bicarb
salt
450 gms. pure ghee

1. Clean and prepare the vegetables. If using tiny papri keep whole and string it from both sides and place in salted water. Cut the brinjals into four and leave intact at the stem and place in salted water. Cut the sweet potato into thick slices, and the yams into 1¼" pieces. Soak all three separately in salted water. Wash the bananas and slice at the end of the preparation. Slit the tendlis into fine strips and soak in salted water.

2. Grind the masala to a soft paste with a little water.

3. Prepare the muthias by placing the gram flour in a bowl. Add salt, fenugreek leaves, washed and finely chopped, onion, a pinch each of turmeric, soda or baking powder, the lime juice and sugar. Mix well and with the help of a little water – half a cup or so – make a stiff dough. Make even sized balls, about 20 to 25, and take each in your right hand and form in the shape of a fist. Heat a little ghee in a small kadhai and fry over medium flame till golden brown. Set aside.

Sambhariya Bheeda   (104
Masoor   (113
Tittori   (113
Vengna Na Simla Mirchi Nu Salnoo   (108
Keri Nakheli Chana Ni Dar   (114
Chora   (112
Patrel   (99

4. Boil the papri in salted water, drain and set aside. Deep fry the baby brinjals, tendlis, kamodio kand, sweet potatoes and yam, separately, till cooked. Pressure cook the beans with salt, a pinch of turmeric and when cooked drain in a colander.

5. Take a large vessel and put the ghee in which the vegetables had been fried. Heat over a medium-low flame and add the ajwain seeds, curry leaves, turmeric, sambhar masala and asafoetida and after two minutes add the ground masala and any left over ghee if necessary. Cook the masala over a low fire for seven to ten minutes, add two cups of water and when the gravy boils add the vegetables in this order, beans, papri, yam, tendli, muthias, sweet potatoes, kamodio kand and lastly the fried bananas with their skins on. Stir very carefully so as not to break up the vegetables and hold the vessel with both hands and shake it from side to side. Allow to simmer for 20 minutes and then serve after tasting for salt.

Sali-Ma-Marghi (12)
Khimo-Sali-Vatana-Sathe (81)

PAPRI
(Broad Bean Vegetable)

Preparation Time: 15 mins.
Cooking Time: 40 mins. • Serves 4-5

300 gms. papri
3   large ripe tomatoes
2   large onions
1   bunch green garlic
2   split green chillies
1   bunch coriander
$\frac{1}{2}$ pod garlic
4   sweet potatoes, boiled
1   teaspoon ajwain seeds
1   tablespoon ginger, chopped
1   tablespoon chilli powder
$\frac{1}{2}$ teaspoon turmeric powder
3   tablespoons oil or ghee

1. Remove stalks from the papri, wash and cut each pod into the desired number of pieces. Wash thoroughly once again.

2. Put four cups of water in a medium sized vessel. Bring to boil. Add salt, turmeric and lastly the vegetable. Allow to cook on an open stove till soft. Do not drain the water.

3. Chop the onion finely. Slice the sweet potatoes and cut the tomatoes into small pieces. Wash the green garlic and cut finely.

4. In a clean vessel heat the ghee. When hot add the ajwain seeds, chillies and the chopped ginger and garlic. Lower the flame and fry till the ginger browns. Add the tomatoes and chilli powder. Cover and simmer over a very low flame for five minutes. Stir and add the sweet potatoes and the vegetable with whatever water that is leftover after boiling it. Mix well with the masala and cover and simmer for 15 minutes. Garnish with chopped coriander and serve with kababs and rotlis.

LAGAN-SARA-ISTEW

(Vegetable Stew)

Preparation Time: 1 hour
Cooking Time: 1 hour • Serves 8-10

1   cup boiled double beans or val papri
1   cup carrots, finely diced
1   cup sweet potatoes, finely diced
1   cup yam, finely diced
1   cup potatoes, finely diced
1   cup lady fingers, finely sliced, deep fried
1   cup french beans, finely diced boiled
1   cup green peas, boiled
1/4 cup vinegar
1/2 cup black currants or raisins
1/4 cup sugar
4   large onions
4   large tomatoes
1/4 bunch coriander
2   teaspoons ginger, chopped
2   teaspoons turmeric powder
1   tablespoon chilli powder
1/2 cup dates, stoned chopped
1/2 teaspoon nutmeg-cardamom powder
2   teaspoons pepper powder
1   teaspoon carraway seeds, roasted
     salt
     ghee

1. Apply salt to the carrots, potatoes, yam and sweet potatoes and deep fry them separately. Drain and remove. Lightly salt and fry the boiled french beans.

2. Soak the black currants in vinegar and sugar. Chop the coriander and tomatoes and keep aside. Reserve some fried lady fingers and green peas.

3. Chop the onions and fry in four tablespoons of the leftover ghee till brown. Add the chopped ginger, turmeric and chilli powders, pepper, carraway seeds, nutmeg-cardamom powder and salt. Add two tablespoons more of the ghee, the tomatoes, coriander and after five minutes add all the fried vegetables, double beans, the boiled green peas, the soaked currants, dates and the vinegar mixture. Stir back and forth till the vegetables have absorbed all the masala. Cover and keep on a low heat for 20 minutes. Top with the reserved peas and lady fingers.

GALKA YA GHEE TOORIA NI TARKARI

(Cooked Sponge Gourd)

Preparation Time: 12-15 mins.
Cooking Time: 20-25 mins. • Serves 4-5

500 gms. tooria
200 gms. onions, chopped
2   tomatoes, chopped
1   teaspoon ginger-garlic paste
1/2 teaspoon cumin seeds, roasted
     salt
     oil

1. Peel the skin of the tooria with a sharp knife and cut into small pieces.

2. Place onions in a saucepan with some oil and allow to cook till pink. Add the cumin seeds and ginger-garlic paste and fry well. Add the tomatoes, salt and tooria and cover the vessel and allow the vegetable to cook in its own juice over a very slow flame.

TARKARI NI KARI

(Vegetable Curry)

Preparation Time: 35-40 mins.
Cooking Time: 35-40 mins. • Serves 6-8

150 gms. potatoes cut into cubes
100 gms. green peas, boiled
100 gms. carrots cut into small pieces
75 gms. french beans cut into small pieces
200 gms. tomatoes
6 drumsticks cleaned and cut into 3" pieces
$1/2$ coconut, grated
12 ressampatti red chillies
1" piece fresh turmeric
10 large garlic cloves
50 gms. whole coriander seeds ⎱
25 gms. khaskhas seeds ⎰ grind
25 gms. sesame seeds together
50 gms. dalia or skinned grams in half
50 gms. skinned salted cashewnuts cup water
10 black peppercorns
2 onions skinned and chopped
2 sour limes, juice removed
1 sprig curry leaves
oil
salt

1. Cut all the vegetables and soak them in water. Chop tomatoes finely and set aside. Grind the coconut masala till soft. Boil the drumsticks in salted water till soft. Drain the water.

2. Place one cup of oil in a dekchi and drop the curry leaves in it. When the oil starts smoking add the ground masala and lower the flame and fry till red. Add the vegetables; chopped tomatoes and salt to taste and cook for five minutes more. Then add four tea cups of water and bring to a fast boil, lower the flame and allow to simmer till vegetables become soft and tender. Add the boiled drumsticks and the sour lime juice.
If you are using the curry with rice you may add more water and make it thinner.

CHAAS PAYELO SAKARKAND

(Caramelised Sweet Potatoes)

Preparation Time: 5 mins.
Cooking Time: 25 mins. • Serves 4-6

300 gms. long, thick sweet potatoes
1 cup sugar
1 cup jaggery-mashed or grated
3 cardamoms seeds
1 teaspoon vanilla essence
1 cup water
ghee

1. First boil the sweet potatoes and skin them. Then slice into two from top to bottom and cut each half into three pieces. You can cut thick slices if you wish.

2. Place the sugar in a saucepan along with the jaggery on a slow fire and allow the sugar to brown lightly and then add one cup water and cardamom seeds and make a sticky syrup. Keep stirring till the mixture boils. Remove from the fire and add the vanilla essence.

3. Take a frypan half full with ghee. Heat the ghee and when it's hot, fry the sweet potatoes till they are golden. Remove with the help of a perforated spoon and place the potatoes directly in the syrup. Shake the pan and allow the potatoes to absorb the warm syrup.

4. Serve along with your breakfast dishes or at meal times.

NARIEL NA DUDH MA RANDHELU CAULIFLOWER

(Cauliflower Cooked in Coconut Milk)

Preparation Time: 10 mins.
Cooking Time: 30-35 mins. • Serves: 5-7

1	kg. cauliflower sprigs
2	large coconuts, milk removed
250 gms.	onions, chopped
5	large, whole Kashmiri chillies with stems intact
1	garlic pod
2	bay leaves
2	1" pieces of cinnamon
2	cardamoms coarsely beaten with a ladle
4"	piece celery
4	tomatoes skinned and deseeded
	oil for cooking
	salt to taste

1. Wash the cauliflower sprigs well and check that no worms adhere to it. Place the finely chopped onions in a pan and add ½ cup oil and fry till golden brown.

2. Add the garlic cloves coarsely crushed, the spices and whole chillies and lower flame. Then toss in the cauliflower sprigs, tomatoes and the celery cut into 1" pieces. Cover and allow to simmer over a low flame with 1 cup water. When the water has dried up add the salt, pepper and coconut juice and keep cooking over a low flame till the juice has all been absorbed.

SAMBHARIYA BHEEDA

(Lady Fingers Cooked in Sambar Masala)

Preparation Time: 22 mins.
Cooking Time: 25-30 mins. • Serves 6

500 gms.	tender green lady fingers
250 gms.	onions, chopped
300 gms.	tomatoes, skinned and deseeded
2	tablespoons coriander, chopped
2	tablespoons fresh coconut, grated
1	sprig curry leaves
1	tablespoon Gujarati pickle sambar powder
1	teaspoon turmeric powder
1	teaspoon Kashmiri chilli powder
1	tablespoon coriander seeds dried, coarsely ground
1	teaspoon cumin seed coarsely ground
	oil
	salt to taste

1. Wash the lady fingers. Top and tail them. Cut into one inch pieces. Apply salt and set aside.

2. Place the chopped onions in a vessel alongwith half a cup of oil. Cook over a medium flame till pale brown in colour. Toss in all the spices and the coconut and fry well. When well mixed add the curry leaf and tomatoes. Cover and cook over a slow flame. Do not allow to burn.

3. Half fill a kadhai or frying pan with oil, and when the oil is nice and hot, fry the lady fingers in small batches and place in a colander. Sprinkle fine salt on the fried lady fingers.

4. When all the lady fingers have been fried toss them in the coconut mixture and stir.

5. Heat over a slow flame and serve with hot parathas.

THE UBIQUITOUS BRINJAL

Brinjals come in all colours and sizes. They are purple, purple black, green and white, purple and white and even a deep pinkish colour. They are tiny and globular, medium and globular, long and spindly and large, U shaped and fat and they can all be cooked in various ways, fried, steamed, braised, baked, curried and mashed. I am particularly fond of this vegetable and it turns up very frequently at our dining table. I like to eat it cooked with prawns but even better when they are baked with cheese sauce and paneer. This is an uncommon dish and I have never eaten it as yet in anyone's house.

JEENA VENGNA PANEER SATHE BHUNJELA

(Baked Baby Brinjals)

Preparation Time: 22 mins.
Cooking Time: 20-30 mins. • Serves 6

12	baby brinjals, halved horizontally with stem attached
200 gms.	fresh punjabi paneer very finely chopped
150 gms.	any good cheese grated
$1/2$	litre milk
2	tablespoons cornflour
$1/4$	teaspoon nutmeg powder
3	tablespoons butter
1	pinch sage
	salt

1. Soak the halved brinjals in salted water after scooping the flesh from the centre with a sharp knife.

2. Mix the cornflour in three tablespoons of water, add to the milk with two tablespoons of butter and cook over a medium flame till a thick white sauce or roux is made. Add 50 gms. cheese and taste for salt. Mix in the nutmeg powder and sage.

3. Remove the brinjal pieces from the salted water and pat them dry with a cloth. Stuff as much paneer as you can in each hollow. Cover with the sauce and sprinkle the grated cheese.

4. Grease a tray with the remaining tablespoon of butter and arrange the brinjal pieces on it. Heat oven to 375°F and place the brinjals in the oven after ten minutes. Bake till the brinjal topping is golden brown.

VAGHARELI FARAJ BEEJ

(Sauteed Frenchbeans)

Preparation Time: 30 mins.
Cooking Time: 20 mins. • Serves 4

300 gms. long, tender frenchbeans
3   green chillies
2   large onions
3   large tomatoes skinned and deseeded
$1/2$ teaspoon broiled, coarsely ground cumin seed
$1/2$ teaspoon mustard seeds
1   teaspoon red chilli powder
1   teaspoon turmeric powder
10   garlic cloves
1   teaspoon sesame seeds, roasted
       oil
       salt

1. Wash and string the beans and cut finely in a diagonal fashion. Slice the garlic cloves and chop the onions and tomatoes.

2. Take a pan and place a quarter cup of oil in it. Put in the mustard seeds and sesame seeds and allow to splutter after which put in the onions and chopped chillies, lower the flame and cook till the onion is soft. Then add the washed sliced beans, the masala powders and garlic and stir well. Add one cup water, lower the flame, cover the pan and allow to cook.

3. Keep stirring the pan every few minutes so that the vegetable does not burn. After it is half cooked, put in the tomatoes after pulping them. Cover and cook over a very low flame till tender. If necessary add water as needed.

4. I normally cook the frenchbeans in a pressure cooker. Add 1 teaspoon sugar if desired before serving the beans.

CHANA NI DAR MA DODHI

(White Gourd cooked in Chana Dal)

Preparation Time: 12 mins.
Cooking Time: 25 mins. • Serves 5

300 gms. white gourd
100 gms. gram (pulse)
2   large onions
3   large tomatoes
$1/2$ cup coriander, finely chopped
4   green chillies finely chopped
2   sprigs of curry leaves
$1^{1}/_{2}$ teaspoons Parsi dhansakh masala
1   teaspoon garam masala
1   teaspoon chilli powder
$1/2$ teaspoon turmeric powder
1   tsp. ginger-garlic paste
       oil
       salt

1. Skin the gourd, deseed it and chop into tiny cubes. Chop the onions and tomatoes finely.

2. Place the chopped onions and half cup oil in a pressure cooker. When the onions are soft and pink add the curry leaves; all the spices and ginger-garlic paste. Stir well, lower the flame and add the green coriander, chillies and tomatoes. Wash the dal twice and add it to the cooker. Add salt and three cups of water and the chopped vegetable. Close the cooker and cook till the vegetable and gram dal are soft.

3. Serve with fried fish and parathas.

VENGNA-NA-BHAJIYA
(Brinjal Bhajias)

Preparation Time: 15 mins.
Cooking Time: 18-20 mins. Serves: 6

2	large brinjals-skinned
2	sour limes juice removed
1	teaspoon chilli powder
1	teaspoon turmeric powder
1	teaspoon jeera, coarsely ground
1	teaspoon ginger-garlic paste
$1/_4$	teaspoon black pepper, coarsely ground
	salt to taste

For the Batter

$1^1/_2$ cups gram flour
$1/_2$ teaspoon cooking soda or baking powder
1   teaspoon chopped fresh coriander
1-2 cups water
    salt to taste
    oil for frying

1. Skin the brinjals and slice them. Mix in a thali with salt, lime juice and all the masalas.

2. Heat a fry pan or kadhai with oil.

3. Make a batter with 1 cup water, the gram flour, coriander, salt and soda. Taste for salt. Add more water if required.

4. When the oil starts smoking, dip a few slices at a time in the batter and fry till golden brown.

VENGNA-NA-CUTLES
(Brinjal Fritters)

Preparation Time: 15 mins.
Cooking Time: 20 mins. • Serves: 6

2	large black brinjals – skinned	
2	tablespoons white vinegar	
6	Kashmiri chillies	
1	tablespoon white sesame seeds	grind together
$1/_2$"	piece ginger	in $1/_4$ cup
2	tablespoons ground nuts or cashew nuts	water
3-4	eggs	
	bread crumbs	
	salt	
	oil for frying	

1. Skin and slice the brinjals. Prick with a fork and marinate in salt and vinegar for two hours.

2. Grind the masala finely with a little water and apply it to the slices.

3. Heat a fry pan with oil. Coat the slices with bread crumbs and arrange on a thali.

4. When the oil smokes, beat the eggs well, dip each slice separately in the egg mixture and fry in batches of 4-6 depending upon the size of your fry pan.

    Do not fry over a high flame as the brinjal slices might remain undercooked.

RAVAIYA

(Chutney Stuffed Brinjals)

Preparation Time: 20 mins.
Cooking Time: 20-25 mins. Serves: 4

6-8 small brinjals (should be tender and without
    seeds about 4" in size)

1/2	coconut	
9	red chillies	
1	teaspoon coriander seeds	grind
1	teaspoon khaskhas-poppy seeds	together
1	teaspoon cumin seeds	in 1/4 cup
1	tablespoon channa or grams	water
1	tablespoon groundnuts	
1	tablespoon tamarind	
1	tablespoon til seeds or sesame seeds	
1/2	teaspoon turmeric til or sesame oil	

1. Grind to a paste the above ingredients
   with one teaspoon salt and keep aside.
   Use water if necessary.

2. Wash the brinjals and wipe dry and cut
   crosswise from the bottom taking care to
   keep the brinjal whole at the stem. Apply
   salt and turmeric powder to the brinjals
   on both sides. Divide the masala into as
   many portions as there are brinjals and
   carefully stuff them taking care to see
   that the mixture does not ooze out. Tie
   with white string.

3. Take a large frying pan or kadhai and
   put in 2-4 serving spoons of oil and heat.
   When the oil smokes, put in the brinjals
   and fry quickly on both sides. Lower the
   flame and add 1/2 cup water in which half
   teaspoon of salt has been dissolved.
   Cover and cook, turning over the brinjals
   so that both sides are cooked. If
   necessary add extra water.

4. The brinjals must be soft and tender
   when served and no water must remain
   in the pan.

VENGNA NE SIMLA MIRCHI NU SALNOO

(Brinjal Capsicum Salan)

Preparation Time: 7 mins.
Cooking Time: 20 mins. • Serves: 5

500 gms. brinjals cut into 1" chunks
200 gms. capsicums, chopped into squares
250 gms. tomatoes, finely chopped
200 gms. onions, finely chopped
2   tablespoons fresh coriander, chopped
1   teaspoon turmeric powder
1   teaspoon chilli powder
1 1/2 teaspoons dhansakh masala
1/2 teaspoon garam masala
1/2 cup tomato ketchup
    salt to taste
    oil

1. Place the chopped capsicum and brinjal
   pieces in salted water. Deep fry the
   brinjals, drain and place in a tray.

2. Cut the onions finely and place in a pan
   with half a cup of oil. Cook till soft and
   pink and drain the oil. Add chopped
   tomatoes, masalas, salt, and the ketchup
   and cook till you get a smooth pulp over
   a low fire. Add the brinjals and shift the
   pan from side to side and allow to
   simmer for five minutes.

3. Heat the oil in which the brinjals had
   been fried on a high heat. Drop the
   capsicum pieces in the hot oil and
   remove immediately. Drain and place
   over the brinjals. Garnish with the finely
   chopped coriander.

KACCHA TAMBOTA MA VENGNA

(Brinjals cooked with Raw Tomatoes)

Preparation Time: 20 mins.
Cooking Time: 40 mins. Serves: 6-8

250 gms. brinjal, skinned and cut into pieces
200 gms. raw tomatoes
100 gms. onions finely chopped
1   tablespoon sliced garlic
2   tablespoons coriander, chopped
1   tablespoon mint, chopped
1   teaspoon coriander seeds
$1/_2$ teaspoon cumin seeds, roasted
3   whole Kashmiri chillies
$1/_2$ teaspoon turmeric powder
1   teaspoon sambar masala
2   tablespoons jaggery, crushed
1   sprig curry leaves
   salt
   oil

1. Place brinjal pieces in salted water. Wash tomatoes and cut each into four pieces. Place onions with two tablespoons oil in a pan. Cook over a low fire till onions are pink. Add brinjal pieces, cover and cook for two minutes. Add tomatoes alongwith half cup water and allow to simmer till brinjals are cooked. This will take twenty-five minutes. Add water if necessary. Taste for salt.

2. Take a frying pan, add two tablespoons oil. Place on medium heat, add curry leaves, garlic and chillies. Fry for two minutes, lower flame, add coriander and cumin seeds. Cook for two minutes, the jaggery, turmeric and sambar powder and stir non-stop. Add two tablespoons water and a quarter teaspoon salt. Cook for two minutes and add the mixture to the brinjals and tomatoes. Simmer for seven minutes. Serve garnished with mint and coriander.

VENGNA NU BHARAT

(Brinjals cooked with Yoghurt)

Preparation Time: 40 mins.
Cooking Time: 20 mins. Serves: 4-5

2   large black brinjals
1   cup curd
6   green chillies
6   black peppercorns
1   pod garlic   ⎫ grind
1   tablespoon cumin seeds   together
1   tablespoon white poppy seeds
$1/_2$ cup cashewnuts ⎭
1   tablespoon sugar
1   bunch spring onions
$1/_2$ cup green coriander leaves, chopped
1   sprig curry leaves
   1 cup oil
   salt

1. Grease the brinjals with oil and poke a skewer through them. Light a small sigri with coals. When the coals are red hot, bake the whole brinjals over the fire taking care not to burn the outer skin. When you feel that the insides have become soft, remove the skin and make a pulp of the white flesh. You can do the same over a gas stove.

2. Chop the spring onions and fry them in half a cup of oil with the curry leaves. When the onions become soft and pink add the finely ground masala and cook over a slow flame. When an aroma arises from the masala, toss in the brinjal pulp and cook well till the oil starts separating from the vegetable. Remove from the fire.

3. Whip the curd along with the sugar and add it to the cooked vegetables. Taste for salt and serve sprinkled with fresh, finely chopped coriander.

PAPETA NA SADA PATTICE

(Potato Cakes)

Preparation Time: 20 mins.
Cooking Time: 25-30 mins. Serves: 7-8

6   potatoes, boiled, mashed
3   carrots, boiled, mashed
1   cup green peas, boiled, mashed
$1/2$ teaspoon turmeric powder
1   teaspoon Kashmiri chilli powder
1   teaspoon toasted coarsely ground cumin seeds
1   teaspoon pickled green pepper, coarsely ground
2   tablespoons coriander, freshly chopped
2   tablespoons sour lime juice
2   tablespoons sugar
4-6 fresh eggs
2   cups bread crumbs
     salt
     oil

1. Take a large thali or tray and mix all the ingredients, except the last four, together. Mix well. Salt to taste.

2. Wet your hands and make twenty equal portions and shape into small round pattice. They should be flat at top and bottom. You can make larger or smaller sized pattice according to your choice.

3. Place the bread crumbs on a wooden board and cover the potato cakes all over with them.

4. Heat a kadhai or fry pan with oil and dip the crumbed cakes in the beaten eggs. Deep fry till golden brown.

KHAMAN PATTICE

(Potato Balls stuffed with freshly grated coconut)

Preparation Time: 35 mins.
Cooking Time: 40 mins. Serves: 8-9

1   kg. potatoes, boiled mashed
1   coconut, grated
1   tablespoon ginger, grated
1   tablespoon chopped green chillies ⎫ grind together
1   teaspoon black peppercorns
2   tablespoons fresh coriander, chopped
$1/4$ cup seedless raisins, washed
$1/4$ cup charoli, washed
2   tablespoons lime juice ⎫ mixed with
2   tablespoons sugar
6   eggs
     bread crumbs
     salt
     oil

1. Mash the potatoes with a little fine salt, make into a round ball and set aside.

2. Grind the ginger, green chillies and black pepper and place in a bowl. Add the grated coconut, coriander, raisins, charoli and the lime juice and sugar. Mix well. Add salt to taste.

3. Divide the mashed potato into even sized balls. Oil your palms and flatten the potato in your palm into a circle. Fill it with the khaman mixture and shape it into a pattice.

4. Roll the pattice into the bread crumbs. Beat the eggs and set a kadhai half filled with oil to heat.

5. When the oil is hot, dip the pattice into the beaten eggs and fry in very small batches of four to five, till golden brown.

KACCHA TAMOTAMA DOUBLE BEEJ

(Double Beans Cooked in Raw Tomatoes)

Preparation Time: 10 mins.
Cooking Time: 1 hr. • Serves 25-30

300 gms. dried double beans soaked overnight in water
250 gms. raw tomatoes
200 gms. onions cut finely
1/2 coconut, grated ⎫
1 tablespoon ginger-garlic paste ⎬ grind finely with 1/4 cup water
4 red chillies ⎬
4 green chillies deseeded ⎬
1 tablespoon cumin seed ⎭
1/2 teaspoon turmeric powder
3 teaspoons Parsi dhansakh masala
3 tablespoons crushed jaggery
salt
oil

1. Soak the double beans overnight in plenty of water. Next day remove them from the water and wash twice. Place them in a pressure cooker with half a teaspoon of turmeric, salt to taste and six cups of water. Cook till tender.

2. Place the chopped onions in a large dekchi and cook in half a cup of oil till golden brown. Add the ground masala, dhansakh masala and jaggery, lower heat and cook for five minutes to seven minutes.

3. Wash and cut the tomatoes into small pieces and add them to the masala. Allow to simmer for fifteen minutes. Strain the water from the double beans and discard it. Toss the beans in the masala-tomato mixture. Simmer for twelve minutes. Mix well and serve.

SEKTA NI SING MA TOOVAR DAR

(Masala Dal with Drumsticks)

Preparation Time: 10 mins.
Cooking Time: 35 mins. • Serves 6

350 gms. toovar dal
6 drumsticks
1 onion, chopped
1 large tomato
6 large green chillies
1 bunch coriander
2 sprigs curry leaves
1 1/2 teaspoons ginger-garlic paste
1 1/2 teaspoons turmeric powder
2 1/2 teaspoons chilli powder
2 teaspoons dhanajeera powder
2 tablespoons jaggery
3 tablespoons ghee
salt to taste

1. Clean drumsticks and cut each into four equal sized pieces. Tie four pieces together with a string and boil the bundles in salted water till cooked. When done, drain out water and keep aside.

2. Wash the dal and put it in the pressure cooker or on a stove together with the salt, turmeric, chilli powder, chopped onion, half the coriander, green chillies and ginger-garlic paste. When cooked pass the dal through a sieve if necessary.

3. Put the ghee in a clean vessel and when hot add curry leaves, dhansakh masala and finely chopped tomato and the boiled drumsticks. Stir from side to side and then add the jaggery and sieved dal. Cover and allow to simmer over a low flame for at least half an hour. Serve sprinkled with the reserved coriander.

CHORA

(Black Eyed Beans)

Preparation Time: 15 mins.
Cooking Time: 30 mins. • Serves 6

These are my mother's favourite pulses and she likes the way I cook them.

300 gms. dried chowli beans
$1/2$ coconut, grated ground fine
1 teaspoon garam masala
1 tablespoon ginger-garlic paste
1 tablespoon chilli powder
1 tablespoon dhansakh masala
1 teaspoon turmeric powder
3 medium sized onions
4 large tomatoes
$1/2$ cup chopped coriander
1 teaspoon sugar
ghee
salt

1. Soak the chowli beans for 2-4 hours or overnight.

2. Chop the onions finely and place them in a pressure cooker along with three-four tablespoons of ghee. Allow onions to cook till golden, and then add the ground coconut, all the masalas, sugar, tomatoes and coriander. Stir constantly and when the tomatoes start to soften wash the soaked beans and add them to the cooker. Add salt and four cups of water.

3. Close the cooker and allow to cook till soft and tender.

LAL RAJMA NI DAR

(Rajma Dal)

Preparation Time: 10 mins.
Cooking Time: 40 mins. • Serves 4-5

300 gms. rajma beans soaked overnight in water
$1/2$ coconut, milk removed
1 tablespoon ginger-garlic paste
$1^1/2$ teaspoons chilli powder
1 teaspoon turmeric powder
1 teaspoon sambar powder
1 teaspoon Parsi dhansakh masala
4 tomatoes, chopped
2 onions, chopped
100 gms. jaggery
salt
ghee

1. Soak the rajma beans overnight. This makes them swell and they are easier to cook. Wash twice the next morning.

2. Place the rajma in a pressure cooker along with the turmeric powder, ginger-garlic paste and five cups of water. Add salt to taste and cook till soft.

3. Take a heavy vessel and place half a cup of oil in it. Place the chopped onions in the oil and cook till soft and pink. Add all the spice powders, and lower the flame. Add the tomatoes and allow to soften. Add the cooked beans along with the coconut milk. Stir well, add the jaggery and allow to simmer slowly till only a thick gravy and the beans remain.

TITTORI

(Sprouted Bitter Beans)

Preparation Time: Indefinite
Cooking Time: 40 mins. • Serves 6

Sprouted vaal beans are considered a delicacy by the community. This is a speciality dish where the Vaal pulse is kept in a damp cloth for 3 days and nights till it sprouts. On the fourth morning, the outer skin must be removed by hand and the pulse must be washed twice carefully. If 300 gms. are soaked they become 600 gms. in weight when you cook them. This dish is always eaten with rice rotlis and dried Bombay duck patia and comes from the Parsi villages of Gujarat.

300 gms. dried vaal soaked for 3 days to sprout
1   coconut, milk removed
$\frac{1}{2}$ dried kopra
$1\frac{1}{2}$ tablespoons Parsi dhansakh masala
1   tablespoon garam masala
1   tablespoon chilli powder
1   teaspoon turmeric powder
4   large onions
4   large tomatoes
1   tablespoon ginger-garlic paste
1   tablespoon sugar
       oil
       salt to taste

1. Wash the vaal dal twice and set aside.

2. Grind the dry coconut finely with the help of half a cup of water. Grate the fresh coconut and with 2 cups hot water put it in a mixer to obtain thick coconut milk. Strain and set aside. Throw away the squeezed coconut.

3. Chop the onions and tomatoes finely. Place the onions, ginger-garlic paste in a wide mouthed dekchi. Cook in one cup oil till soft and then add the finely ground dried kopra, spices, sugar, salt and the tomatoes. When the masala has cooked add the sprouted dal, coconut

milk and two cups water and allow to cook till soft. The dal should remain intact and not disintegrate so do not stir, but shake the vessel from side to side. Add more water if needed and allow to simmer till soft. Taste for salt and remove from heat.

MASOOR

Preparation Time: 10 mins.
Cooking Time: 20 mins. • Serves 6

350 gms. masoor or black lentils
2   small onions
1   bunch spring onions
4   large tomatoes
1   teaspoon ginger-garlic paste
1   teaspoon turmeric powder
2   teaspoons red chilli powder
$1\frac{1}{4}$ tablespoons dhansakh masala
$\frac{1}{2}$ cup tamarind water
       jaggery the size of a large lime
3   green chillies, finely chopped
$\frac{1}{2}$ bunch coriander, finely chopped
2   sprigs curry leaves
       salt to taste
       oil

1. Wash the lentils and place them in a pressure cooker along with the turmeric, ginger-garlic paste and salt. Cook till soft.

2. Chop the onions, spring onions finely and cook them in oil till soft in a large pan. Add the green chillies, curry leaves, tomatoes finely chopped, chilli powder and dhansakh masala. Once the mixture is cooked and the oil separates, add the tamarind water, jaggery and stir for five minutes. Add the cooked lentils, coriander and stir for two minutes. Simmer on a low flame for ten minutes and serve with rotlis and onion kachumbar.

KERI NAKHELI CHANA NI DAR

(Chana Dal with Raw Mangoes)

Preparation Time: 10 mins.
Cooking Time: 25 mins. • Serves 4-5

300 gms. chana dal or gram dal
100 gms. raw mangoes
150 gms. spring onions
100 gms. tomatoes
1 tablespoon ginger finely chopped
1 bunch green coriander
1 teaspoon turmeric powder
1 teaspoon Kashmiri chilli powder
1 tablespoon Parsi dhansakh masala
4 green chillies-finely chopped
  salt
  oil

1. Wash the chana dal twice.

2. Chop the spring onions finely and place in a large pan with half cup oil. Cook till soft. Add the chopped ginger, green chillies, spice powders, and tomatoes. When the tomatoes begin to soften add the washed chana dal, salt and three cups of water and allow to cook on a medium flame uncovered till soft. Add more water if necessary.

3. Just before serving mix in the washed finely chopped coriander and peeled, chopped raw mangoes and keep over a very slow flame till the mangoes are soft.

4. Serve with hot rotlis.

TOOVAR NI DAR

(Pigeon Peas)

Preparation Time: 15 mins.
Cooking Time: 35 mins. • Serves 4-6

300 gms. toovar dal
2 onions
2 potatoes
4 tomatoes
6 green chillies
1/2 bunch fresh coriander
1 tablespoon roasted peanuts
·1 teaspoon roasted sesame seeds ⎫
1 teaspoon cumin seeds ⎬ grind together in water
1/2 teaspoon poppy seeds ⎭
6 Kashmiri chillies
1/2 teaspoon turmeric powder
1 teaspoon amchur powder
3 tablespoons ghee
  salt

1. Chop the onions finely and fry in a heavy bottomed vessel in three tablespoons ghee. When golden brown add the ground masala, turmeric masala and fry for three minutes, then add tomatoes, green chillies and coriander.

2. Peel and chop the potatoes into fine cubes. Wash the dal twice. Then add both items to the onion mixture along with four teacups of water and cook over a medium flame till tender and soft. You can place the dal in a pressure cooker if you like - it will become soft and tender faster than if cooked in a vessel.

3. Add the amchur powder, stir, allow to heat for 5 minutes and serve.

SUNNA-NA-DANA-NO-PULAO

(Golden Beads Toovar Dal Pulao)

Preparation Time: 25 mins.
Cooking Time: 1 hour. • Serves 8

This is an old Parsi favourite totally forgotten by the present generation. I have yet to eat this delicious dish in anyones house.

500 gms. basmati rice
2 gms. saffron
6 cloves
10 black peppercorns   }
2" cinnamon   } whole
3 green crushed cardamoms   } masala
2 bay leaves   } for the
2 star anise   } rice
1 coconut, milk removed
3 cups toovar dal
1½ cups thick curd or yoghurt
2 teaspoons sugar
2 onions, fried, sliced
2 onions, chopped
4 potatoes, cubed
1 carrot, sliced
3 tomatoes, skinned and
  chopped
1 cup green peas, boiled
6 green chillies deseeded and
  chopped.   } for the
3 tablespoons fresh coriander, } toovar
  chopped   } dal
2 tablespoons fresh mint,
  chopped
2 tablespoons ginger-garlic paste
2 tablespoons garam masala
1 tablespoon chilli powder
1 teaspoon turmeric powder
2 cups ready made wheat flour
  dough
  salt
2 cups pure ghee

1. Cook the rice in an electric rice cooker or set a large pan of salted water to boil. Add a quarter cup of pure ghee, the whole spices and boil rice till cooked. Drain in a colander.

2. Heat the saffron on a tava and crumble it in half a cup of boiling water. Allow to steep for fifteen minutes and pour over the cooked rice. Stir the rice and lay it out in a thali to cool.

3. Wash the toovar dal and boil it with turmeric powder and salt in extremely hot water. Allow to cook till soft – the dal seeds should remain intact. If they disintegrate, your pulao will be a failure. Drain in a colander.

4. Take two chopped onions and one cup ghee and place it on medium flame in a flat bottomed pan. Allow to cook till soft and pink. Add the ginger-garlic paste, the cubed potatoes, the sliced carrot and cook till soft by adding the coconut juice. When the potatoes soften add the chilli powder, garam masala, cooked green peas, chopped tomatoes, green chillies, fresh coriander and mint and stir gently for a further seven minutes. Slowly fold in the boiled toovar dal and gently mix into the gravy with a saucer.

5. Take a large biryani handi and place a little ghee at the bottom. Then put half the boiled rice at the bottom. Cover the boiled rice with the toovar dal mixture and then place the remaining half of the rice over it. Cover with the two fried onions.

6. Whip the yoghurt with two teaspoons of sugar and cover the top of the rice with it. Cover the dekchi with a lid or foil and then pinch it to the edge of the vessel with the dough. Make a long rope of the dough and see that the vessel is air tight. Place over an extremely low flame or coal sigri and allow to come to dum. Open only after half an hour.

MUNG NI DAL NE PAPETA

(Moong Dal with Potatoes)

Preparation Time: 10 mins.
Cooking Time: 25 mins. • Serves 6

350 gms. yellow skinned moong dal
2   large onions
4   large potatoes
4   large tomatoes
1$\frac{1}{2}$ teaspoons chilli powder
1   teaspoon turmeric powder
$\frac{1}{4}$ fresh coconut grated ⎫
15   cloves garlic   ⎪
1"   fresh ginger piece   ⎬ grind finely
4   green chillies   ⎪
1"   piece cinnamon   ⎭
     salt
     ghee

1. Wash the moong dal thrice. Peel and cut the onions and potatoes into small cubes and wash once and place the items in a vessel along with the turmeric, salt and four cups of water. Cook till soft.

2. Grind the coconut, chillies, ginger-garlic and cinnamon with a little water.

3. Heat half a cup of ghee and fry the ground masala and chilli powder well for three minutes. Add half a cup of water and bring to a boil, then add the cooked dal and tomatoes and stir lightly. Simmer on a low flame for five minutes before serving.

TARKARI NI KHICHDI

(Rich Vegetable Khichdi)

Preparation Time: 20 mins.
Cooking Time: 30 mins. • Serves 7

300 gms. fine basmati rice
50 gms. masoor dal
$\frac{1}{2}$ cup onions, sliced deep fried
1   teaspoon carraway seeds
1$\frac{1}{2}$ teaspoons turmeric powder
10-15 peppercorns
2" cinnamon pieces
6-8 cloves
3-4 bay leaves
2   large onions, chopped
1   large tomato, sliced
250 gms. each: sweet potatoes, carrots and lady fingers, chopped fine, salted and fried.
100 gms. green peas, boiled, salted
1   coconut, thick milk removed
$\frac{1}{2}$ cup coriander, chopped
    salt to taste
    pure ghee

1. Fry the chopped onions, carraway seeds, pepper, cinnamon, cloves and bay leaves in two serving spoons of ghee and when lightly done add the washed rice and dal, turmeric and salt. Cover with sufficient water so that the grains are completely cooked. When the water has evaporated add the fried onions and boiled vegetables and the coconut milk. Mix, cover tightly and keep on a low flame till completely cooked. When serving sprinkle with coriander leaves and decorate with sliced tomatoes.

Tam-Tamta-Gos-Na-Kabab   (83)
Gor-Aamli Ni Kachumbar   (131)
Keri-Nu-Pani-Nu Achaar   (122)
Bapaiji Ni Dhansakh Ni Dar   (7)
Dhansakh Na Vagharela Chaval (118)
Keri Mewa Nu Achaar   (127)

MEVA NE TARKARI NO PULAO

(Dried Fruit and Vegetable Pulao)

Preparation Time: 15 mins.
Cooking Time: 45 mins. • Serves 6

350 gms. basmati rice
100 gms. cashewnuts
100 gms. raisins (large)
100 gms. dried apricots soaked in water overnight and halved
200 gms. potatoes
100 gms. green peas
1 tablespoon fresh mint, chopped
2 large onions
2 large tomatoes, skinned, deseeded
$^1/_2$ cup yoghurt
2 gms. saffron
2 tablespoons sugar (optional)
1 small piece cinnamon
2 cardamoms
8 black peppercorns
1 mace flower
1 teaspoon carraway seeds
   salt
   ghee

1. Wash the rice twice and set aside. Chop the onion finely and place in a large pan which has a well fitting lid. Add three tablespoons ghee. When the onion turns golden put in the whole spices and the washed rice and fry lightly. Add salt and four cups of water and boil the rice on high for ten minutes. Then lower the flames, cover lightly and allow to simmer. Do not close the lid tightly but allow it to cover three quarters of the pan. After fifteen minutes mix the rice with a fork and test for water. If more water is necessary keep adding half a cup of warm water at a time. Cover and remove from the fire as soon as the rice is cooked.

2. Peel the potatoes and cube them. Deep fry and set aside. Boil the green peas in water along with salt and one tablespoon chopped fresh mint.

3. Place the yoghurt and sugar in a bowl and whisk well till the sugar has dissolved. Chop the tomatoes very fine and add to the yoghurt.

4. Cook the apricots with one teaspoon sugar and the water in which they were soaked. Fry the cashewnuts and raisins.

5. Open the pan of rice and lightly mix in the fried potatoes, boiled peas, the apricots without their syrup, the raisins and cashewnuts. Lastly mix in the yoghurt mixture. Toss the rice lightly and then heat the saffron on a skillet. Take the hot strands between your fingers and mix into the rice. Stir the rice lightly till the saffron is evenly distributed, then cover the pan tightly with foil.

6. Heat in an oven or over a very low flame for fifteen minutes before serving.

Gos Na Cutles (82)
Tamtamta Gos Na Kabab (83)
Kismis Khima Na Pattice (79)
Bheja-Na-Cutles (70)

KAJU SAATHE KHICHDI PULAO

(Luscious Khichdi Pulao)

Preparation Time: 20 mins.
Cooking Time: 40 mins. • Serves 8

500 gms. basmati rice
$1/2$ teaspoon turmeric powder
$1/2$ cup onion slices, deep fried golden brown
2 whole pieces of cinnamon
4 cloves
2 cardamoms coarsely beaten
2 kala elchas
2 whole badiyaan
2 javantri flowers
10 black peppercorns
2 coconuts, milk removed
2 capsicums thinly sliced
$1/4$ cup raisins
5 green chillies ground
$1/4$ cup whole cashewnuts
$1/2$ cup green peas, boiled
$1/2$ cup french beans and carrots, boiled
use pure ghee if possible otherwise use oomda or dalda

1. Wash the rice well. Heat the fried onions in a little ghee and add the whole spices, turmeric, salt, little water and bring to a quick boil. Add the rice. Immediately keep on simmer and when rice is half cooked add the milk of 2 coconuts and the ground green chillies. Add the milk carefully — a little at a time till the rice cannot absorb more. Cook covered over a very low flame till tender. Taste for salt. This rice is best made in an electric rice cooker as the grains do not stick.

2. Heat $1/2$ cup pure ghee and lightly fry the capsicum strips, raisins and cashewnuts. Set aside. Add the boiled vegetables to the same pan and holding the pan with both hands swirl them around and gently mix into the cooked rice.

3. Decorate the khichdi with fried capsicum, raisins and cashewnuts.

DHANSAKH NA VAGHARELA CHAVAL

(Dhansakh Whole Spice Rice)

Preparation Time: 10 mins.
Cooking Time: Approx. 35 mins. • Serves 6-8

50 gms. sugar
500 gms. long grained rice
2 onions
3 cardamoms
3 cloves
10 peppercorns
$1/2$ teaspoon carraway seeds
3 bay leaves
1-2 small pieces cinnamon
1 teaspoon cumin seeds
salt to taste
3 dessertspoons pure ghee

1. Caramelise the sugar by heating it. Add a quarter cup of water and mix well.

2. Wash the rice twice and set aside.

3. Chop onion finely and fry in three dessert spoons of pure ghee till brown. Add the cumin seeds, the other spices and the caramelised sugar water. When a nice aroma is emitted put in the washed rice and salt. Add water and bring to a boil. Lower the heat. Cover till done. Do not stir the rice unnecessarily. The grains must remain intact.

4. The best results are obtained by putting the rice in a steam cooker.

CHOKHA NI ROTLI

(Rice flour Rotlis)

Preparation Time: 15 mins.
Cooking Time: Depends upon amount of cooked flour

Rice rotlis are difficult to make. My mother Piroja is an expert and taught me how to make them whilst I was still in school. Everything depends on your experience. You can't make them by using a velan or dough pin. There is no short cut for making chokha ni rotlis. You heat water and add the salt, rice flour and mix it vigorously in the pan till you get a thick large ball of flour without a single lump. Remove from the fire and place in a large thara or kuthrot and using the knuckles of both your hands knead the dough. If the dough is too dry, wet your hands and sprinkle some drops on the dough and knead again till it is smooth and soft. Make a long roll of the dough and place it against the rounded side of the thara or kuthrot. Place an iron skillet or tava on the stove and wipe it with a clean cloth. Take a small scoop of dough, roll it lightly in rice flour, place it on a broad wooden board and pat it into a round with the palm and fingers of your right hand.

The rotli should be patted in such a way that it turns in an even circle and the pressure of your hand is evenly distributed over the roll. The right size would be that of a quarter plate or a little smaller.

If the tava is very hot the rotli will scorch immediately. Temperature is all important. The tava should be hot but not smoky. Place your rotli on it and quickly flip it over with a tavatha or any other spatula. Lightly press the rotli with a clean soft cloth and flip it over again. When you feel that the dough is cooked, remove the rotli and place it on a mulmul cloth or supra. The rotlis must have no yellow or black dabs on it.

KESAR NI ROTLI

(Saffron Rotlis)

Preparation Time: 12 mins.
Cooking Time: 25 mins. Serves: 5

200 gms. flour
75 gms. powdered sugar
20 gms. almonds, boiled skinned, sliced finely
20 gms. pistachios, boiled skinned, sliced finely
150 ml. milk with cream
2 gms. saffron heated on a tava and finely crumbled
    pure ghee

1. Place sieved flour on your work surface and make a hole in the centre. Add saffron, milk and sugar and mix well and knead to a smooth dough.

2. Make about ten balls from this dough. Roll out into a round the size of a small normal roti, apply ghee to the surface and fold into half. Apply ghee again and fold into a quarter triangle. Then roll it out into a roti, press almond and pistachio slices on one side and cook slowly with ghee on both sides.

PAPETA – NA –PARATHA
(Potato Bread)

Preparation Time: 25 mins.
Cooking Time: 45 mins. Serves: 4-6

For the Covering:
250 gms. wheat flour
1-$\frac{1}{2}$ cups water
$\frac{1}{4}$ cup ghee
    salt

For the Filling:
3   large potatoes boiled and mashed
1   teaspoon green chillies, finely chopped
2   teaspoons green coriander, finely chopped
$\frac{1}{2}$ teaspoon black pepper powder
$\frac{1}{2}$ teaspoon amchur powder
$\frac{1}{2}$ teaspoon fennel powder
2   teaspoons pure ghee
    salt
    ghee for roasting the parathas

1. Place the flour in a large thali, add water as needed, ghee and salt and knead well for several minutes till you get a smooth dough. Cover and keep in a cool place.

2. Heat two teaspoons pure ghee in a small frying pan. Drop in the green chillies, pepper, amchur, and fennel powders. Stir and cook for one minute. Add to the fresh coriander, mashed potatoes and salt. Mix well and set aside.

3. Roll the dough out into a long roll, place on a board and divide into twelve equal parts, and keep covered.

4. Take one portion and roll out into a round disc. Apply a little ghee onto half the disc and fold it into a crescent. Apply ghee on half the crescent and fold it into a triangle. Roll out the triangle into a round disc 4-5" in diameter. Place two tablespoons of potato mixture on the disc and spread smoothly over it leaving a half inch of space round the circle edge. Then make another disc in the same manner and cover the disc with the potatoes mixture. Press along edge and seal.

5. Heat the tava and place the paratha upon it. Flick it over onto the other side. Then take one teaspoon of pure ghee and pass it around the paratha. Turn and cook the other side. Press the paratha down with a spatula and turn once again till golden brown. Serve at once with green coconut chutney or chundo.

MITTHI PURI
(Sweet Puris)

Cooking Time: 15 mins. Serves: 4-5

100 gms. semolina
100 gms. maida or self-raising flour
50 gms. castor sugar
$\frac{1}{2}$ teaspoon vanilla
$\frac{1}{2}$ cup rosewater
    pinch of soda-bi-carb
    pinch of salt
    ghee for frying

1. In a large thali sieve the flour, add the semolina, sugar, vanilla, pinch of salt and soda-bi-carb, one teaspoon ghee and mix. Add half a cup of rosewater and knead into a firm dough. Add more water only if necessary. Cover with a damp cloth for half an hour.

2. Make 14 to 20 round balls. Roll them out on a wooden board. Deep fry 4-5 at a time in ghee till they puff up and then remove from the ghee and eat whilst hot.

BUFENU

(Ripe Mango Pickle in Oil)

Preparation Time: 2 days • Preserve for 2 months before use • Serves 10-12

Six large, ripe Alphonso mangoes are the major focus of this very unusual pickle. I've never seen this particular recipe cooked by any other, than a Parsi family. This pickle is a meal in itself and can be eaten alongside a dal or vegetable dish, or if you don't have time to cook you can eat it as an accompaniment to a vegetable or masala khichdi. The following is my mother's recipe.

6	ripe alphonso mangoes
100 gms.	garlic, skinned
12	cloves
200 gms.	mustard powder
2"	piece cinnamon
150 gms.	cumin seeds
350 gms.	jaggery
3	tablespoons chilli powder
1	teaspoon turmeric powder
	sugar cane vinegar
2 kgs.	sesame or til oil
	salt to taste

1. Wash the mangoes and dry them gently with a soft cloth and set aside.

2. Take a large bowl and place the mustard powder in it along with 1 cup of oil and beat well with a spoon.

3. Crush the garlic, cumin, cinnamon and cloves coarsely and set aside. Use half a cup vinegar or dry crush.

4. Place oil in a large vessel on the stove. When the oil becomes hot, drop the mangoes one by one carefully into the vessel. Lower the flame and cook the mangoes in the oil turning them over several times till they are nice and red on the outside. Cover the pan and turn off the stove. Remove mangoes with a slotted spoon and place in a thali.

5. The next day, heat the jaggery and half a bottle vinegar in a saucepan. Allow the mixture to boil well. Then cool it.

6. Take a large thali and pour in all the ingredients such as the mustard and oil mixture, the vinegar and jaggery mixture, the crushed garlic, cumin, cinnamon and cloves and salt to taste. Mix vigorously with the palm of your hand. Add the chilli and turmeric powders also. When the mixture is nice and thick pour in one cup of the oil in which the mangoes were fried. Mix well again.

7. Take a large mouthed tall glass jar. Pour in one cup of the mixture at the base and arrange the six mangoes in the jar. Pour the mixture over the mangoes. They should be totally covered. Cover the mangoes with any leftover oil in which the mangoes had been fried.

8. Eat after two months.

KERI-NU-PANI-NU-ACHAAR

(Mango Pickle in Brine)

Preparation Time: 30 mins.
No Cooking • Serves 40

2½ kgs. tender, small, raw mangoes-whole
½ kg. salt
1 teaspoon hing or asafoetida
20 green chillies
1 tiny knob alum or 1 raised teaspoon after coarse crushing

1. Wash and dry the mangoes. Do <u>not</u> chop them.

2. Take a large brown and white pickle bottle. Put salt at the bottom, then place a layer of mangoes, then salt and again a layer of mangoes with chillies, till all the mangoes are used up. Pour boiled cooled water till the mangoes are inundated.

3. Top the bottle with hing and the alum. Seal and allow the pickle to stand for 2 months before using it.

   Do not get frightened if you see a layer of black fungus when you open the bottle. Shift it aside and remove as many mangoes as you need. Allow the fungus to slide back and pack the bottle securely.

   Wash and slice the mangoes. Eat them with yellow dal and rice.

PANI-NU-KARVANDA-NU-ACHAAR

(Karvanda Pickle in Brine)

Preparation Time: 30 mins.
No Cooking • Serves 50-80

5 kgs. raw karvandas
2 teaspoons green ginger, cut into strips
1 cup whole green chillies with tops intact
1-2 kgs. salt
a small knob of alum half the size of a sour lime
1 teaspoon hing or asafoetida

1. Wash and dry the karvandas.

2. Place salt at the bottom of a large pickle bottle and layer it with karvandas, chillies, ginger strips followed by a layer of salt till the bottle is full. Top it with hing and alum and fill it up with boiled, cooled water. Allow to stand for 2 months before using it.

3. Do not worry if you see a layer of black fungus when you open the bottle. Push it aside, remove the amount of karvandas you want and allow the fungus to settle back. Seal the bottle. Wash and drain karvandas before eating them.

LIMBU-MARCHA-NU-ACHAAR

(Lemon and Chilli Pickle in Oil)

Preparation Time: 1 hr.
No Cooking. • Serves 60-80

5	kgs. sour limes
1	kg. large green chillies (optional)
1/4	kg. red chilli powder
1/4	kg. turmeric powder
2	tablespoons asafoetida powder
2	kgs. salt
3-5	kgs. refined til oil

1. Wash the sour limes, allow to dry and cut into 8 pieces. Remove the seeds as they spoil the taste of the pickle.

2. Combine the salt and powdered masalas. Place a layer of the salt mixture at the bottom of the pickle jar. Then place a layer of sour limes and chillies. Continue to do so till you reach the top of the jar. Close it.

3. For three days, turn the pickle upside down, once a day.

4. On the fourth day heat the oil and cool it. Pour into the jar until it has totally covered the lime pieces. Shake the bottle, stir the pickle and top it with some more oil. Wipe the mouth of the jar, inside and out with a clean piece of cloth. Seal the bottle and use the pickle after 2 months.

5. This pickle is best made in the months of April and May.

PIROJA NU VENGNANU ACHAAR

(Mother's Brinjal Pickle)

Preparation Time: 25-30 mins.
Cooking Time: 30 mins. • Serves 30

1	kg. large black brinjals	
6	green chillies	
2	pods garlic sliced finely	
3"	piece fresh ginger	
1	tablespoon khaskhas	grind in
1	tablespoon (sesame) til seeds	vinegar
1	tablespoon dried coriander seeds	
1	tablespoon cumin seeds	
1	teaspoon mustard seeds	
2	tablespoons chilli powder	
2	tablespoons sugar	
	sugar cane vinegar	
	salt to taste	
	oil	

1. Grind the masala finely with half to one cup vinegar and set aside.

2. Skin the brinjal, chop into small cubes and apply salt.

3. Heat three cups of oil in a large pan. Add cumin and mustard seeds. Fry the masala till golden red. Add the brinjal, chilli powder, sugar and half a bottle of vinegar and cook over a slow fire till brinjals are tender. Mix well, taste for salt, cool and fill the mixture in a large jar.

4. It is ready to eat immediately.

BHING NI GHARUB NU ACHAAR

(Bhing Fish Roe Pickle)

Preparation Time: 40 mins.
Cooking Time: 45-50 mins. Serves: 25-30

12	pieces of double bhing fish roes
250 gms.	red Kashmiri chillies
150 gms.	cumin seeds
150 gms.	coriander seeds
1	tablespoon black peppercorns
150 gms.	garlic
100 gms.	mustard seeds
50 gms.	red chilli powder
1½ kg.	jaggery
2	tablespoons turmeric powder
2½	bottles strong sugarcane vinegar
	coarse kitchen salt as necessary
	til oil

grind in vinegar (red Kashmiri chillies through mustard seeds)

1. Soak the chillies in two cups of vinegar. Grate the jaggery and allow to soak in half a bottle of vinegar.

2. Grind the red chillies, cumin seeds, mustard seeds, coriander seeds, black peppercorns and garlic in the vinegar in which the chillies were soaked.

3. Wash the fish roes in water, then in vinegar. Apply turmeric and salt and boil whole in half bottle vinegar. Cool and cut each roe into four to six pieces.

4. Heat two cups of til oil in a wide mouthed, flat langri. Allow to heat, not smoke and add the ground masala and fry till red. Add the grated jaggery with the vinegar in which it was soaked and the chilli powder and mix well. Allow to simmer for ten minutes before adding the fish roes. Taste for salt. Shake the pan from side to side and allow to cook for a further ten minutes. Cool. Bottle in airtight jars. This pickle can be eaten immediately.

CHAMMNA NU ACHAAR

(Pomfret Pickle)

Preparation Time: 30 mins.
Cooking Time: 40 mins. Serves: 7

2	large pomfrets cut into small pieces
1	bottle sugarcane vinegar
200 gms.	jaggery (optional)
12	Kashmiri chillies
2	pods garlic
2	tablespoons cumin seeds
1	tablespoon mustard seeds
1	teaspoon black peppercorns
1	cup fresh cut coriander
6	deseeded green chillies
1	tablespoon chilli powder
1	teaspoon turmeric powder
	salt
	oil

grind together in vinegar (Kashmiri chillies through deseeded green chillies)

1. Cut each pomfret into small pieces. Wash well, apply salt, turmeric and chilli powder and set aside. Do not use the soft stomach flap portion.

2. Take a frypan and half fill it with oil. Fry the fish pieces in small batches taking care not to bruise them.

3. Grind the masala to a very fine paste with half a cup of vinegar.

4. Heat one and a half cup of oil in a large thick bottomed pan, preferably a langri. Fry the masala well till it is cooked and then add two cups of vinegar and the jaggery and allow to boil for fifteen minutes. When the mixture has cooked and is thick add the fish pieces. Shake the pan from side to side, taste for salt, and remove from the fire. Cool and bottle.

KOLMI-KANDA-TAMOTA NU ACHAAR

(Prawn, Onion and Tomato Pickle)

Preparation Time: 40 mins.
Cooking Time: 45 mins. Serves: 15-20

500 gms. prawns, shelled, deveined
4   finely chopped onions
2   tomatoes, skinned, deseeded, finely chopped
2   tablespoons ginger-garlic paste
12   red Kashmiri chillies
6   green chillies
3   tablespoons roasted cumin
     seeds
3   tablespoons roasted coriander   } grind in
     seeds   vinegar
1   tablespoon roasted
     fenugreek seeds
1   tablespoon roasted mustard
     seeds
1   teaspoon black peppercorns
1   teaspoon asafoetida
2   tablespoons turmeric powder
1   tablespoon amchur powder
2   sprigs curry leaves
1   bottle sugarcane vinegar
1/2 litre sesame oil
     salt

1. Wash and drain the prawns twice. Apply coarse salt, turmeric powder and set aside for an hour. Then place in a flat bottomed vessel and cook till soft in one and a half teacups of vinegar. Cook till prawns are tender.
2. Grind the spices finely with the help of half a cup of vinegar.
3. Take a large vessel and add the two cups of oil. When hot, add the curry leaves, the onion and fry till golden brown. Add the amchur powder, ginger-garlic paste and the ground masala, reduce heat and cook for five minutes stirring all the time. Add one cup vinegar plus the finely chopped tomatoes and cook the liquid for five minutes over a low heat. Add the

cooked prawns and allow the mixture to simmer for ten to fifteen minutes. Cool and bottle. This pickle can be used immediately and should be refrigerated at all times. Use within ten days.

KOLMI NU KHATTU-MITTHU ACHAAR

(Sweet and Sour Prawn Pickle)

Preparation Time: 40 mins.
Cooking Time: 45 mins. Serves: 10

4   cups large deveined prawns
1 1/2 cups jaggery
3   cups sugarcane vinegar
8   green chillies, deseeded slit
1   sprig curry leaves
16   Kashmiri chillies
2   whole pods garlic
3   tablespoons cumin seed   } grind
1   teaspoon mustard seeds   together
1   teaspoon fenugreek or   in half a
     methi seeds   cup of
1   teaspoon turmeric powder   vinegar
1/2 teaspoon badisonf
     oil
     salt

1. Wash the prawns well. Place in a saucepan along with two teaspoons salt, curry leaves, green chillies and two cups of vinegar. Allow to cook well and when prawns are tender – cool.
2. Grind the masala till soft and buttery.
3. Place two cups of oil in a large pan. Allow to heat and then drop in the ground masala and stir non-stop till it is red and gives off a good aroma. Add the jaggery and mix well. When it dissolves in the masala, add the prawn mixture with the vinegar. Simmer for ten minutes. When the mixture is well cooked, cool and fill glass jars.
4. The pickle is ready to eat immediately.

PACHRASIYA ACHAAR NO. 1

(Mixed Vegetable Pickle)

Preparation Time: 1 hour.
Cooking Time 25 mins. • Serves 40-50

500 gms. seedless long black brinjals
500 gms. red carrots
500 gms. red pumpkin
500 gms. raw melons
500 gms. white pumpkin
250 gms. kharak - dried dates cut in halves
250 gms. deseeded black currants
50 gms. fresh ginger thinly sliced and cut into strips
200 gms. fresh large garlic cloves sliced and cut into strips
250 gms. dried apricots – cut into 2 pieces
100 gms. Ahmedabadi large boras
50 gms Kashmiri chilli powder
15 gms. turmeric powder
$1/2$ teaspoon clove powder
1 teaspoon cardamom powder
3 kgs. best quality jaggery
4 bottles sugarcane vinegar
salt – coarse kitchen variety

1. Soak all the vegetables in handfuls of salt in separate vessels. Cut them into sticks. Soak the apricots, dried dates and deseeded black currants in vinegar overnight.

2. Next morning wash all the vegetables lightly in vinegar and place in a colander. Allow all the liquid to drain off.

3. Meanwhile place three bottles of sugarcane vinegar in a large open mouthed dekchi. Crush the jaggery and add it to the vinegar and bring it to a strong boil. Add the vegetables one by one, chopped ginger, garlic and the dried fruits, the boras last of all. Stir carefully so that the vegetables don't get bruised. Boil for five minutes. Taste for salt. Sprinkle the chilli powder, turmeric, and clove and cardamom powder over the vegetables. Stir for two minutes and remove the dekchi from the fire. Cool and fill in clean, dry glass bottles. The pickle can be eaten after a week or ten days.

4. Use vinegar carefully. No synthetic vinegar should be used.

PACHRASIYA ACHAAR NO. 2

(Mixed Vegetable Pickle)

Preparation Time: 40 mins.
Cooking Time 40-50 mins. • Serves 20-30

300 gms. tiny surti papdi or flat beans
300 gms. black, long, seedless brinjals
250 gms. raw melons
250 gms. carrots
50 gms. fresh turmeric
50 gms. fresh ginger
150 gms. garlic cloves
150 gms. dried figs
150 gms. dried deseeded black currants
100 gms. dried Kashmiri chillies
25 gms. mustard seeds
20 gms. cumin seeds coarsely ground
1 kg. best quality jaggery
500 gms. sugar
2 star anise
2" cinnamon
6 crushed green cardamoms
4 bottles sugarcane vinegar
2 kgs. kitchen salt

1. Soak the figs and black currants in vinegar for twenty-four hours.

2. Cut the fresh turmeric and ginger into fine strips one inch long. Peel the carrots and cut into sticks. Peel the melons, remove the seeds and cut into thin one inch strips. Cover all these vegetables in

kitchen salt in separate containers overnight.

3. The next day, slice the brinjals and string the papdi. Boil a large vessel of water and add two cups salt to it. Drop the brinjal slices in it and allow to boil for five minutes. Drain the water and place the brinjal slices upon a white cloth under a fan. Do the same with the papdi.

4. Once the brinjal and papdi are under the fan, grind the chillies, garlic, mustard and cumin seeds with vinegar.

5. Place one bottle of vinegar in a large vessel and allow it to boil. Crush the jaggery and add it to the vinegar along with the sugar. Stir occasionally. Add the masala. When the vinegar mixture comes to the boil add the salt covered vegetables after draining the salt water. Also add the fruit soaked in vinegar and lastly the brinjal and papdi. Allow to boil for ten minutes, stirring gently all the while. Cool and pack in a large, dry, glass jar. Pickle will be ready to eat within one week.

KERI MEWA NU ACHAAR

(Raw Mango and Dried Fruit Pickle)

Preparation Time: 35 mins.
Cooking Time: about 35 mins. • Serves 30-40

2	kgs. raw tender mangoes
2	kg. white sugar
250 gms. raisins	soaked in
250 gms. dried apricots	vinegar
250 gms. kharak or dried dates	overnight
2	tablespoons chilli powder
2	tablespoons powdered black pepper, cloves, cinnamon, cardamom, nutmeg powder
1	teaspoon haldi powder
	sugar cane vinegar
2	tablespoons dried ginger, thinly sliced
2	tablespoons dry garlic, thinly sliced
	salt to taste

1. Skin the raw mangoes and chop into two pieces. Remove the seed and cut into small cubes. Discard the seeds.

2. Soak all the dried fruit overnight, in a glass bottle full of vinegar.

3. Cut the ginger-garlic a day before and dry it in the sun.

4. Take a large vessel and place the mango pieces and sugar in it and place over a slow fire. Add half cup vinegar so that the sugar starts melting easily.

5. Cook the mangoes in the sugar mixture till soft. Then when the chutney is ready add the spices, chilli powder, dried fruits soaked in vinegar and the dried ginger-garlic. Simmer for fifteen minutes. Cool and bottle.

METHIOO
(Mango and Fenugreek Pickle in Oil)

Preparation Time: 45-50 mins.
No Cooking except oil • Serves 50

2   kgs. raw mangoes, washed, cut into pieces,
    dried and deseeded
1/2 kg. coarse kitchen salt
100 gms. mustard seeds coarsely ground
100 gms. Kashmiri chilli powder
250 gms. fenugreek coarsely ground
50 gms. turmeric powder
50 gms. cumin, coarsely ground
5   gms. asafoetida
2   kgs. sesame oil

1. Take a large thali and mix all the salt and
    masalas and spread a layer of this
    mixture at the bottom of a large pickle
    jar. Then spread a thick layer of mango
    pieces and cover with a layer of the salt
    mixture. Do this till all the mango pieces
    are used up.

2. For three days turn the pickle up and
    down. On the third day heat two kgs. of
    sesame oil. Cool and empty into the
    pickle jar till the mango pieces are totally
    submerged. The oil should form a thick
    layer over the mango pieces.

3. Check on the pickle twice a month. It
    should be ready for consumption within
    three months.

MRS. DEBOO NU METHIANOO ACHAAR
(Mrs. Deboo's Methianoo Pickle)

Preparation Time: 1 hour
No Cooking except oil • Serves 100-150

5   kgs. plump raw mangoes of the best quality
750 gms. Kashmiri chilli powder
500 gms. fenugreek (methi) seeds
200 gms. turmeric powder
75 gms. asafoetida chunks ground coarsely
1 1/2 kgs. coarse kitchen salt
5   kgs. til oil

1. Wash the mangoes and allow to dry. Cut
    into half, discard the seeds and cut into
    small pieces of even size.

2. Grind the fenugreek coarsely in a mixie
    or stone pata. Clean the salt of any
    impurities.

3. Mix the chilli, turmeric, fenugreek,
    asafoetida and salt in one cup til oil.

4. Spread a layer of mango pieces on the
    bottom of a large clean pickling jar.
    Sprinkle over with the salted masala.
    Continue layering the pickle with mango
    pieces and the salted masala till
    everything has been used up. Shake the
    jar, seal tightly and keep in a cool dark
    place for three days.

5. On the third day boil four kilos of til oil
    and allow to cool. Shake the pickle jar
    and pour in the cooled oil till it has totally
    covered the mango pieces and floats one
    inch above the mango pieces. Seal
    tightly and cover the mouth with a piece
    of cloth. Examine the pickle for at least
    thirty days from time to time to see that
    the mangoes are submerged in the oil. If
    necessary boil more oil. Cool and add it
    to the pickle.

CHUNDO (NO. 1)

(Grated Mango Chutney)

Preparation Time: 45 mins.
Cooking Time: 20 mins. • Serves 15-18

1   kg. raw mangoes skinned, deseeded, finely
    chopped or grated
1   kg. sugar
1   level tablespoon coarsely ground cumin seeds
1   tablespoon Kashmiri chilli powder
1   tablespoon salt
1/4" asafoetida, piece
1   cup sugarcane vinegar

1. Place the finely chopped mango pieces,
   sugar and vinegar in a heavy bottomed
   dekchi and allow to cook over a medium
   flame. Keep stirring till the mango pieces
   are cooked.

2. Once the mango pieces have softened,
   add the salt, cumin, chilli and asafoetida
   and stir the mixture for five minutes.
   Remove from the flame and cool. Fill into
   clean, dried, glass jars.

CHUNDO (NO. 2)

(Grated Mango Chutney)

Preparation Time: 50 mins.
Cooking Time: Approx. 25 mins. • Serves 100

3 1/2   kgs. raw mangoes, grated or cut into tiny
        pieces
3 1/2   kg. sugar
250   gms. red seedless raisins
50   gms. red Kashmiri chilli powder
4   teacups vinegar
2   tablespoons cinnamon, clove, black pepper
    powder
2   tablespoons chopped garlic
2   tablespoons roasted crushed cumin seeds
5   gms. asafoetida
2   tablespoons salt

Place the grated mangoes, sugar, vinegar
and garlic in a large, heavy dekchi over a
slow fire. Allow the sugar to melt and keep
stirring off and on for twenty minutes. Add
the raisins, salt, chilli and spice powders and
asafoetida and stir vigorously till the syrup
becomes sticky. Remove from the fire and
cool. Store in clean bottles.

KOPRANA DUDH NI KACHUMBER

(Coconut Milk Salad)

Preparation Time: 15-20 mins.
No Cooking • Serves 5-8

300 gms. red onions finely chopped
100 gms. raw mangoes, skinned and finely
    chopped
10 gms. fresh ginger minced finely
1/2 bunch coriander leaves, finely chopped
5   green chillies deseeded and finely chopped
1/2 large coconut grated
    salt to taste

1. Remove thick coconut milk with one cup
   cold water and add all the chopped
   onions, raw mangoes, ginger, coriander,
   green chillies and salt in a bowl. Mix
   thoroughly.

2. If mangoes are not in season add thick
   tamarind juice.

3. This kachumber is best eaten with
   vegetable khichdi and papads.

BAPAIJI NI TAMOTA NI CHUTNEY

(Grandma's Tomato Chutney)

Preparation Time: 20 mins.
Cooking Time: 20-30 mins. • Serves 15-20.

2   kgs. large, red tomatoes
1½   kg. sugar (reduce sugar if desired)
½   cup sugar cane vinegar
1   tablespoon chilli powder
1   teaspoon powder made from black pepper, cinnamon, cardamom and nutmeg
1   teaspoon dried ginger, minced
1   tablespoon dried garlic, minced
1   tablespoon fresh mint, minced
      salt

1. Place the tomatoes in a pan of boiling water for five minutes. Drain the water and peel, deseed and chop tomatoes into large pieces.

2. Place the sugar, vinegar, salt and a cup of water in a large saucepan and heat slowly over a medium flame. When the mixture starts bubbling add the garlic, ginger, spice powders, mint and tomatoes and keep stirring till the mixture thickens. Add as much salt as desired. Taste and if required add more vinegar.

3. When the mixture thickens, fill into jam jars, cool and cover tightly.

4. Always taste for sugar and salt.

NARIEL NI CHUTNEY

(Green Coconut Chutney)

Preparation Time: 30-45 mins.
No Cooking • Serves 6-10

1   large coconut - grated
15-20 cloves of garlic according to personal preference
6   green chillies - deseeded
1   teaspoon cumin seeds
2   sour limes, juice removed
1½   tablespoons sugar
1   tablespoon chopped mint
2   cups coriander leaves, washed and chopped
½   teaspoon black pepper powder
1   teaspoon salt or per taste

Grind all the ingredients very finely on a stone mortar. Add the sugar and lime juice last. Mix well. Serve.

KERI NI CHUTNEY

(Mango Chutney)

Preparation Time: 10-12 mins.
Makes: 1 cup.

4   raw mangoes peeled and chopped
3   green chillies deseeded
1   tablespoon chopped fresh ginger
1   tablespoon chopped garlic
¼   grated coconut
½   bunch fresh coriander leaves
      salt to taste

Grind all the above items finely until soft. Place in a glass bowl and serve with vegetables or dal and rice.

AAMLI NI CHUTNEY

(Tamarind Chutney)

Preparation Time: 30-40 mins.
Makes: 3 cups

1   cup dates mashed to a pulp
1   cup tamarind pulp
1   cup sugar
1   teaspoon chilli powder
$\frac{1}{2}$ teaspoon cumin powder
    salt to taste

Place all the items in a saucepan with a cup of water. Bring to a fast boil, simmer for five minutes strain and allow to cool. Place in a bottle and chill in the refrigerator. Use as needed.

Variation
2   onions finely chopped
2   tablespoons coriander, chopped
Take a cup of the tamarind chutney and add the chopped onions and coriander and serve it as
GOR-AAMLI NI KACHUMBAR.

SAREEA

(Sago Pappads)

350 gms. sago
1   teaspoon cumin seeds, coarsely ground
$\frac{1}{4}$ teaspoon chilli powder
5   pints water
20   banana leaves
     salt to taste

1.   Clean the sago like you do rice and place it in a large vessel. Add water and salt and bring to a boil. Mix vigorously with a wooden spoon and do not allow any lumps to form.

2.   When the sago has become soft add the cumin and chilli powder and remove from the fire.

3.   Grease the banana leaves spread on newspaper and keep them ready before hand and place one tablespoon of sago at a time on them. Pat the mixture into even circles and dry these papads in the sun. When hard, store in air tight bottles.

4.   Deep fry and eat them.

COOVERBAI'S PARSI DHANSAKH MASALA

(Parsi Dhansakh Masala)

Coriander seeds	(Dhana)	500 grams
Cumin seeds	(Jeera)	250 grams
Kashmiri chillies	(Marcha)	100 grams
Turmeric	(Haldi)	100 grams
Cinnamon	(Taj)	100 grams
Cloves	(Lavang)	100 grams
Black peppercorns	(Kalamiri)	50 grams
Nagkesar	(Nagkesar)	50 grams
Dried ginger	(Soonth)	50 grams
Black Cardamom	(Elcha)	50 grams
Mace	(Javantri)	25 grams
Mustard seeds	(Rai)	50 grams
Poppy seeds	(Khaskhas)	50 grams
Nutmeg	(Jaifal)	2 grams

Grind all the above items to a fine powder and seal in air-tight bottles.

ADU-LASAN

(Ginger, Garlic Paste)

250 gms. ginger
225 gms. garlic
a few grains of coarse salt

Skin the garlic, scrape the ginger and slice it. Grind both into a fine paste without water. If kept in a cool place it will last for a fortnight.

Garam Masala (1) For Rice
broil and grind coarsely and bottle
20   gms. star anise
25   gms. cinnamon
25   gms. clove
100 gms. black peppercorns
15   green cardamoms
10   mace flowers

Garam Masala (2) For Mutton-Chicken-Vegetables
broil lightly and grind finely
50   gms. tamalpatta
25   gms. cloves
50   gms. cinnamon
75   gms. black peppercorns
30   gms. shahjeera
50   gms. mace
25   gms. green cardamom
1   nutmeg